JULIAN H. GONZALEZ

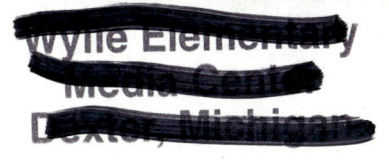

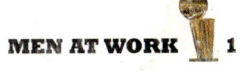

MEN AT WORK 1

REGINA H. BOONE

THE 2004 NBA CHAMPIONS
MEN AT WORK

6 | THE FIRST SHIFT
THE REGULAR SEASON

24 | THE SECOND SHIFT
PROFILES OF CHAMPIONS

56 | THE THIRD SHIFT
FIRST 3 ROUNDS OF PLAYOFFS

92 | THE FINAL SHIFT
THE NBA FINALS

118 | SCOREBOARD & GALLERY

Detroit Free Press

600 W. Fort St.
Detroit, MI 48226
www.freep.com

© 2004 by Detroit Free Press.
All rights reserved.

Manufactured by Quad/Graphics, West Allis, Wis., United States of America.

No part of this book may be reproduced or transmitted in any form or by any means, electronic or mechanical, including photocopying, recording or by an information storage system, without permission of the publisher, except where permitted by law.

Other recent books by the Free Press:

Life After Baseball
Life Lessons
Portraits of War
Razor Sharp:
   Drew Sharp
Hang 10
Time Frames
The Detroit
   Almanac
HeartSmart Kids
   Cookbook
State of Glory
The Corner
PC@Home

Fishing Michigan
Hockey Gods
Motoons:
   Mike Thompson
Ernie Harwell:
   Stories From
   My Life in
   Baseball
Corner to Copa
Century of
   Champions
Believe!
Stanleytown

➤ To order any of these titles, please call 800-245-5082 or visit
www.freep.com/bookstore

➤ To subscribe to the Free Press, call 800-395-3300.

Men at Work:
The book staff

Editor: Mark Francescutti

Designer: Christoph Fuhrmans

Photo editor: Diane Weiss

Photo technicians: Rose Ann McKean, Jessica Trevino

Copy editors: Bill Collison, Matt Fiorito, Maureen Ground, Tim Marcinkoski, Jeff Juterbock, Steve Schrader, Lee Snider and the Free Press sports desk

Project coordinator: Dave Robinson

Sports editor: Gene Myers

Director of photography: Nancy Andrews

Design director: Steve Dorsey

Graphics: Kofi Myler

Special thanks: Brad Betker, Terrance Collins, Owen Davis, Laurie Delves, Bob Ellis, Eric Habermas, A.J. Hartley, Sharilyn Hufford, Ryan C. Moloney, Tom Panzenhagen, Katina Revels, Shelly Solon, Kelly Solon, Al Toby.

Cover design: Rick Nease, Steve Dorsey

Cover photo: Kirthmon F. Dozier

Back cover photo: Mandi Wright

MEN AT WORK 2

Job won

After Goin' to Work every day, Pistons receive their reward

Confetti flies and fans erupt after Detroit's victory in Game 5 of the Finals. The scene at the Palace of Auburn Hills was scary loud.

By Mitch Albom

AUBURN HILLS (JUNE 15, 2004) — They attacked all night, the way you attack a fire, the way you attack an enemy hill, no counting on luck, fate or chance, just sheer will and your own pounding lungs, drive the rim, drive the lane, until finally the horn sounded to end their eight-month shift, which began in October and ended one week shy of summer.

Rip Hamilton was jumping in place, a ball of energy. Mehmet Okur was hugging Tayshaun Prince. Ben Wallace took the spray paint and marked the last game with a big old "X." The team whose motto is "Goin' to Work" had put in a little overtime, and the once-mighty Lakers hadn't just been defeated, they had been stomped and crushed like Italian grapes.

The Pistons didn't just beat L.A., they reduced it to a single letter: "L," as in loser. And as the music soared at the Palace, the Pistons soared right with it.

Pay dirt.

"Never stop dreaming," said Chauncey Billups, the series MVP, smiling widely after the raucous 100-87, Game 5 victory that clinched the NBA title.

Never stop dreaming. But when you wake up, you'll notice a new crown in town. It wasn't stolen. It didn't fall from the sky. The Lakers didn't squander it, and the referees didn't conspire it. The Pistons — write this verb down — won it. Got that, Phil? Got that, Shaq and Kobe? They won it. They captured it. They grabbed it right from Game 1 and owned everything but 11 seconds and one overtime period in what some are referring to as the NBA's

MEN AT WORK 3

Pistons owner Bill Davidson won his third professional sports title in a year. The WNBA's Detroit Shock and NHL's Tampa Bay Lightning, both owned by Davidson, also won championships.

JULIAN H. GONZALEZ

first "five-game sweep."

Along the way, they broke the mold of NBA championship teams. In the final, crowning 48 minutes, Detroit ran dynamite under the Lakers' ego and blew it to shreds. From Billups' game-opening drive to a late Ben Wallace put-back slam, the team-oriented Pistons slam-dunked the superstar era, ripped up conventional wisdom and threw a bucket of paint on the portraits of four future Hall of Famers, who, for this season, will be remembered as all the things the Pistons were not: greedy, selfish, whiny and discombobulated.

The Pistons, meanwhile, were five bodies and 10 hands at a time. And all their hands are on a trophy now. Detroit is back atop the basketball world after 14 years.

"I'm very fortunate to coach this team," a humbled Larry Brown said. "They play the right kind of basketball."

Pay dirt.

What's left to prove? For pete's sake, they led at one stage by 29 points! And from the tip, the Pistons showed maturity beyond expectations. Long shots were passed up. Short shots were passed up. If it wasn't a lay-up or a slam, they didn't want it. They scored more than half of their points (52) in the paint. On one play, Prince leaped twice for a loose ball and was already moving to the hoop before he even had control. He finished with a slam. That was typical.

So much for the moment overwhelming them. They made the Lakers look old and slow. The fact is, the Lakers' best attitude came from Jack Nicholson, who played trash talk with the big screen. Unfortunately for the Lakers, Jack's only slightly older and slower than they are.

Some will call this the biggest upset in the history of the NBA. How amazing is it? Well, remember, the series was preordained as the Lakers vs. "the other guys." The Pistons were supposed to be mindful of their station. "Forget what happened before," pundits kept saying. "This game, you'll be put in your place."

They were. Their place is on the victory stand.

Hooptown, now. There were gas stations in the Detroit suburbs selling Pistons paraphernalia out of small tents, and cars on the highways flying Pistons flags from their windows. The Motor City has big new wheels, orange with laces, and kids everywhere will be growing out their Ben Afros and nicknaming themselves "Rip."

Nothing given. Everything earned. They hit pay dirt in a way that every laborer and sports fan alike can admire. Take a picture of that final moment — Ben spray-painting where X marks the spot — and frame it for next year, above a modified slogan:

Goin' to Work . . .

As the Boss.

Photo on following page by CHIP SOMODEVILLA

Chauncey Billups carries his MVP trophy through the tunnel after the Pistons beat the Lakers. Billups joined Joe Dumars (1989) and Isiah Thomas (1990) as Piston Finals MVPs.

MEN AT WORK 4

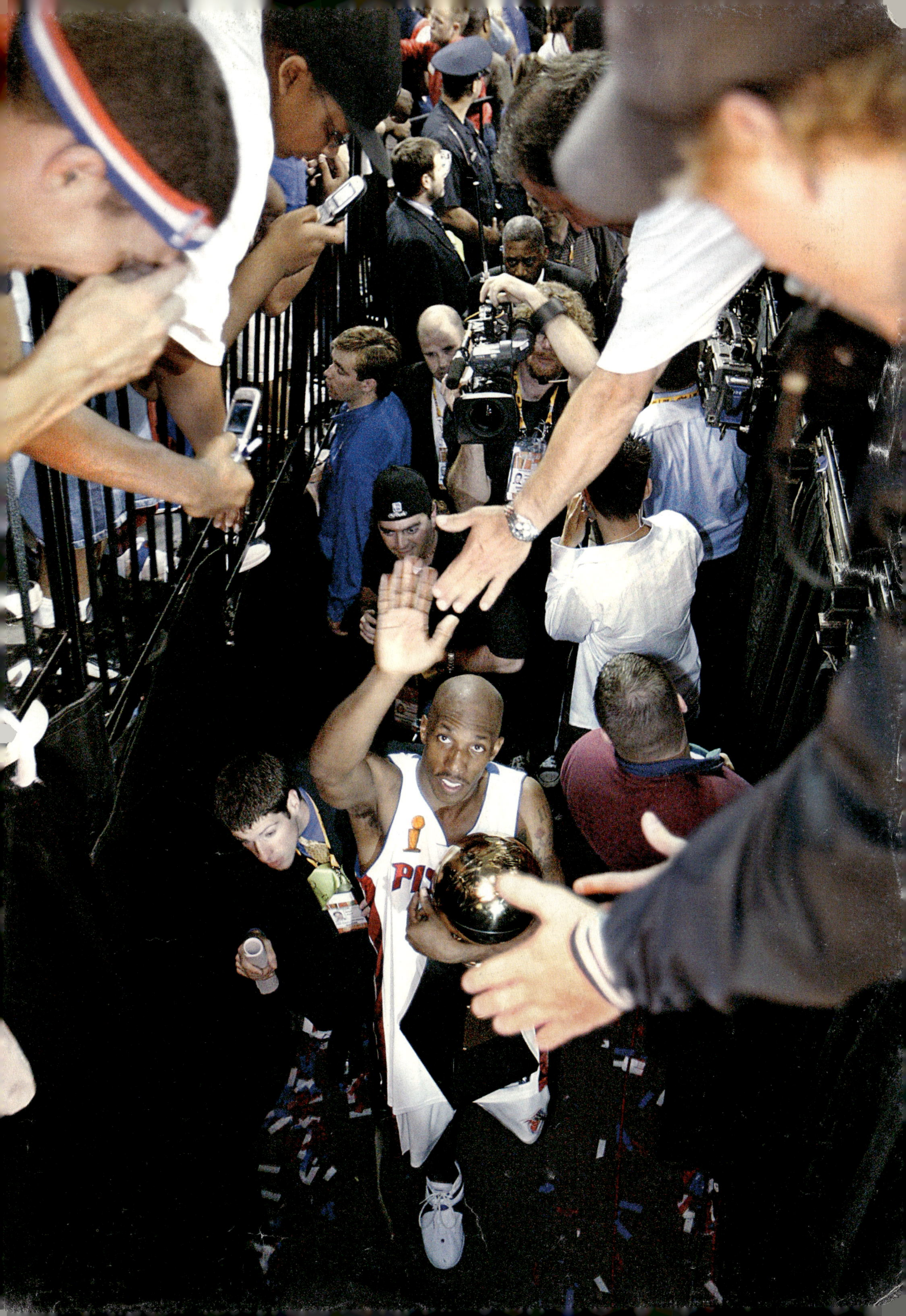

THE FIRST SHIFT

THE REGULAR SEASON

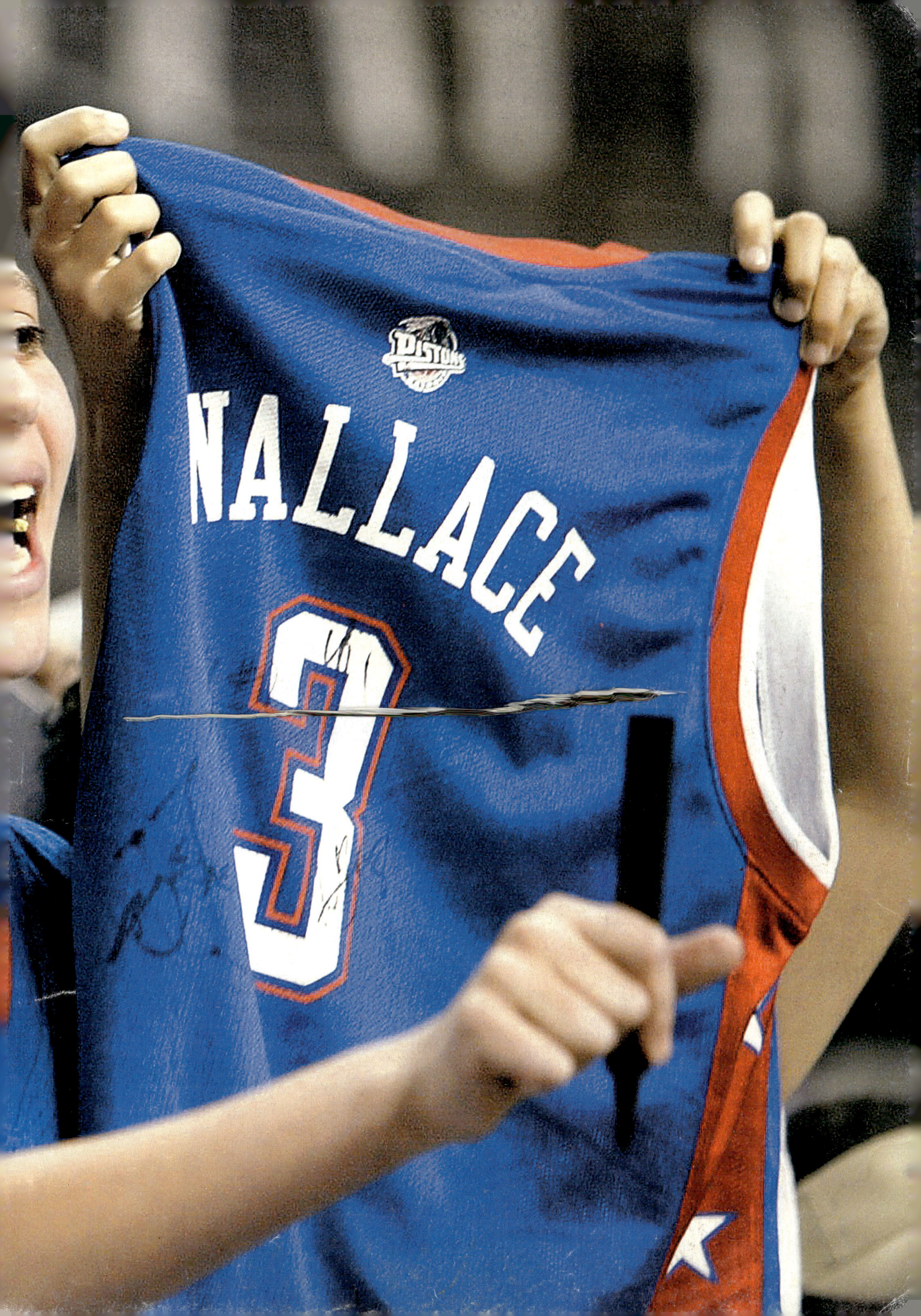
PISTONS
NALLACE
3

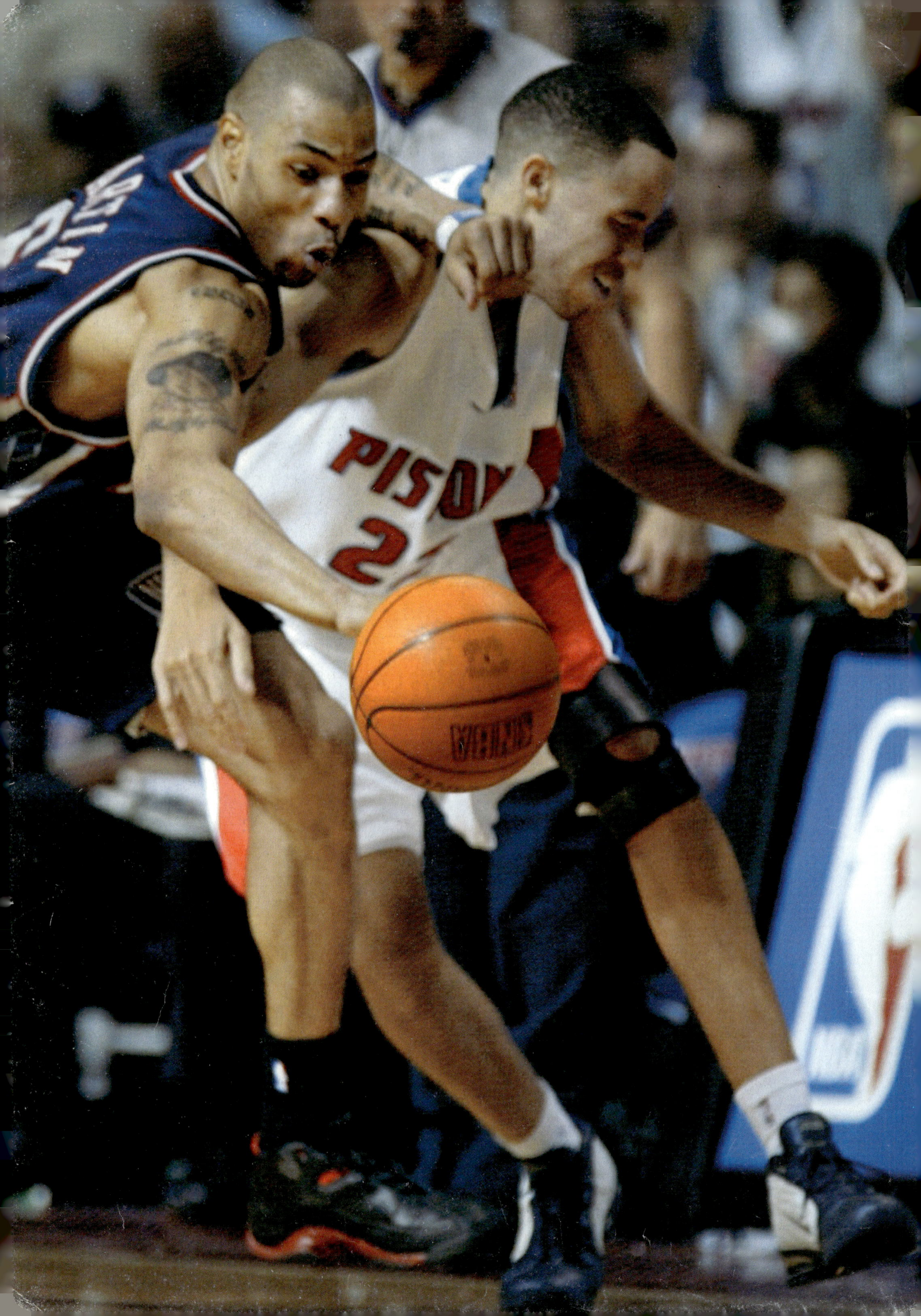

Sweep and weep

New Jersey ends '02-03 Pistons' season in East finals

From left, Tayshaun Prince, Cliff Robinson and Chauncey Billups have front-row seats as New Jersey sweeps the Pistons in Game 4.

By Mitch Albom

EAST RUTHERFORD, N.J. (MAY 24, 2003) — Say thanks and so long. It's over, and it wasn't very good. The Pistons spent most of this series choking on the dust of the streaking Nets. Jason Kidd should have gotten five speeding tickets. His whole team was in overdrive. New Jersey is a state that is famous for its turnpike. I didn't know it ran through the middle of the arena.

What exit do the Pistons get off? They have met their Waterloo.

By the end, players were biting their lips and holding their heads in their hands. Tayshaun Prince looked as if he was going to cry. Michael Curry threw an arm around him for comfort.

"Did it feel as if you were playing at two different speeds?" Corliss Williamson was asked.

"Two different speeds, two different efforts, two different intensities," he sighed.

Also-rans.

Chauncey Billups' sore left ankle prevented him from keeping up with Kidd, who continues to run circles around the guards.

"It felt good to get out there and run," Kidd said.

We're glad he's happy. But the Nets were faster than the Pistons at just about everything — breaks, rebounding, loose balls, finding open shots.

Before Game 3, the Pistons had hit a personal jackpot by claiming the No. 2 pick in the upcoming draft. Some of the Pistons heard this and held up two fingers just before tip-off.

Who knew they were predicting where they would finish?

"We're not playing as a team," Ben Wallace said. "We played as a team to get here and we're not doing that now."

No, they're not. Defensively, they have no answer for Kenyon Martin. They seem incapable of stopping a break (that's effort as much as anything else). And their no-offense thing is truly brutal to watch. It's not just that the Pistons aren't shooting, they aren't running any plays effectively. Everything seems telegraphed. Everything seems labored. They run the shot clock down to the danger zone. They get few offensive rebounds.

The Nets, to a player, acted as if they were on a mission. "What we talked about all season long," coach Byron Scott said, "was getting back to the finals and winning the championship."

The Pistons will need to do that now. Their mantra will be to get back to the Eastern Conference finals and win them. You crawl before you walk.

Photo on opposite page by KIRTHMON F. DOZIER
New Jersey's Kenyon Martin muscles Tayshaun Prince out of the way in Game 2 of the 2003 Eastern Conference finals.

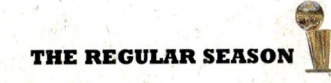

Photo on previous pages by ROMAIN BLANQUART
A new, raucous breed of Pistons fans watched their team win their first title in 14 years.

Carlisle clocks out

Coach fired despite two 50-win seasons

What once seemed like a great partnership came to an abrupt end May 31, 2003, when Joe Dumars fired Rick Carlisle as Pistons coach.

The parting was a very public affair, as Carlisle and Dumars both faced the press at the news conference announcing the coach's dismissal.

By Drew Sharp

AUBURN HILLS *(MAY 31, 2003)* —Rick Carlisle's gradual fall from grace within the Pistons' power sanctum and subsequent dismissal was surprising only to the uninformed.

The forces that brought us to Larry Brown becoming the Pistons' 24th coach were evident but categorically dismissed by outsiders who were blinded by the winning.

You don't have to believe what you choose not to see.

Nobody's more guilty of this than Carlisle. His assistants alerted him of the danger signs, warning him that his personality conflicts with executives and players might cost him his job. But Carlisle brashly assured them that the organization couldn't touch him because of the forward strides in his two years at the helm.

Winning 100 games in two years doesn't heal all wounds.

Carlisle alienated far too many people within this organization with his frequently churlish behavior and obstinate coaching approach.

He ticked off the wrong people, starting with owner Bill Davidson, to whom Carlisle hadn't spoken one word for months.

Carlisle treated certain factions of the organization with utter disrespect, fueling the perception that he considered the Pistons merely a pit stop on his career path. He wasn't going to be here long, so why should he care how he treated others? He rejected the overtures to improve his communication and teaching skills, particularly with younger players.

Carlisle would not have lasted beyond Christmas before a players revolt relaunched his television career and left the Pistons with no alternative but to elevate an assistant coach to an interim post.

This was a breakdown between coach and players, and although it's convenient to assail pampered millionaires for their selfishness, one of the realities of NBA coaching is that control has its limits. Carlisle wanted to script every second of a 48-minute game. You can teach and torment to the point of suffocation,

THE FIRST SHIFT 10

but eventually a coach must trust his players' instincts and their willingness to incorporate the lessons imparted upon them.

"That was always a difficult thing," admitted guard Chucky Atkins. "He didn't speak to a lot of people. When you treat people bad, it comes back to haunt you. If you can't talk to your coach, who can you talk to?"

If team president Joe Dumars believed in Carlisle's capacity to learn from his mistakes, the coaching carousel wouldn't have taken another revolution with the Brown hiring. Dumars could have persuaded Davidson to ride it out for one more year, if he truly believed it was warranted.

But too many bridges had been burned, too many sensibilities had been offended, too many concerns remained. The Pistons contacted Brown, who had stepped down from the Sixers' job, through back channels.

Why commit your future to a man who's a charter member of the Bekins Moving Co.'s coaching Hall of Fame?

To finish the job Carlisle began.

Carlisle responds

Rick Carlisle was a guest on ESPN Radio's "Dan Patrick Show," right after Larry Brown's hiring. His comments:

■ **Was he fired after Brown agreed to come to Detroit?**

"It may have happened that way.... If you're in the Pistons' position and you're going to fire a guy like Rick Carlisle, who's had some success for the last couple of years, you've got to have somebody ready to step in there.... If you're them, and you have a chance to hire Larry Brown, I'm not sure if I can argue with that either."

■ **On reports that personality clashes led to the firing:**

"I've been there two years and a lot of this, quite honestly, blindsided me.... I just choose not to respond to that stuff.... This is the first I've heard of most of this stuff, so my question is, where was all this stuff while I was there?"

"That was always a difficult thing. He didn't speak to a lot of people. When you treat people bad, it comes back to haunt you. If you can't talk to your coach, who can you talk to?"
— Pistons guard Chucky Atkins

KIRTHMON F. DOZIER

Rick Carlisle and his wife, Donna, leave the Palace practice facility after attending the news conference that ended his Pistons career.

Hello, Larry

Brown plans to teach, mold contender

Larry Brown answers questions from the media with Joe Dumars at his side during a news conference announcing his hiring.

By Helene St. James

AUBURN HILLS (JUNE 2, 2003) — First and foremost, Larry Brown wants to teach. His ability to make teams better has made him a respected coach in the NBA, and it convinced the Pistons he would be the perfect choice to mold a good nucleus into a contender.

Capping a 72-hour marathon that began with an inquisitive call to Brown's agent and led to the firing of Rick Carlisle, president Joe Dumars introduced Brown as the franchise's 24th head coach.

Brown, a member of the Basketball Hall of Fame, had already taken six NBA teams to the playoffs, but he hadn't won a championship.

"The biggest goal I have here is, we've got a lot of great young kids that I think I can make a difference, in terms of teaching them how to play and the right way to play," Brown said. "I'm hopeful this franchise can play at a high level for a long time. That's my challenge."

Brown signed a five-year deal worth as much as $30 million with incentives. He resigned from the Philadelphia 76ers a week before joining the Pistons. His departure came 10 days after his Sixers had been eliminated by the Pistons in the second round of the playoffs.

With Carlisle, the NBA coach of the year two years ago, the Pistons went to the second round of the playoffs in 2002 and advanced to the Eastern Conference finals last season. Nonetheless, Dumars fired Carlisle.

Brown is renowned for his knowledge of the game as well as his ability to pack his bags. The Pistons are the seventh NBA team Brown has coached, and Brown is the third coach Dumars has hired since he took over as president of basketball operations in June 2000.

"My personal feeling is that (Brown) is the preeminent coach in the league," Dumars said.

Said Brown: "I've never inherited a team with a winning record. This franchise had everything anybody could be looking for. It's going to give me the greatest opportunity I think I have to make a difference, and I'm looking forward to that."

He vowed Detroit would be "my last stop" on a journey that already has lasted 31 years and now reached its ninth city, but he has thought the same about every previous job.

With a teacher like Brown, there always is one caveat.

"I'm here for the long haul," he said. "As long as I feel I'm helping."

OUTSOURCING — NBA-STYLE:
Why draft American?

Joe Dumars went for height in his three 2003 draft picks: 6-foot-6 Carlos Delfino, 7-foot Darko Milicic and 7-1 Andreas Glyniadakis. Are these the magic numbers for the Pistons? Notice that 24 plus 31 equals 55.

By Drew Sharp

AUBURN HILLS (JUNE 26, 2003) — This wasn't an evening for the phonetically challenged.

It took as long to pronounce the names chosen in the NBA's annual summer shopping spree as it did to draft them.

Whatever happened to the days of Joe Smith?

Is there enough room in the program to write the name Sofoklis Schortsanitis, or perhaps you know him by his more familiar reference (SOF-fik-klees skorts-sa-NEE-tis)?

It's now about Darko and Zarko. It's about scouting Poland, Greece, Brazil and Russia.

The Pistons went the international route in the 2003 draft, not surprisingly taking 7-foot Serbian Darko Milicic (MILL-a-chitch) second overall, but also grabbing swingman Carlos Delfino with the 25th selection. That the 6-6 Delfino was still around that late in the first round stunned the Pistons brass; they figured the 21-year-old Argentina native would have been taken in the top 20.

Some of the ignored American players, who once entertained dreams of shaking commissioner David Stern's hand on the draft podium, are screaming foul.

Sounds familiar, doesn't it? That was the lament of the American autoworkers 25 years ago who branded consumers as traitors or unpatriotic for buying Japanese cars, resulting in the closing of U.S. plants and the loss of jobs.

The lesson finally learned was: Improve the basic quality of the product and the consumers' tastes will change.

Perhaps the lesson for the young American basketball player now is: Improve the basic quality of your game and the tastes of general managers and coaches will change.

A record eight players were taken from foreign teams in the first round. That was part of the

The top picks

1. Cleveland   LeBron James
2. Detroit   Darko Milicic
3. Denver   Carmelo Anthony

OTHER PISTONS PICKS
Who: Carlos Delfino, No. 25 pick.
Position: Guard/forward.
Ht/wt: 6-feet-6, 230 pounds.
Skinny: Born in Argentina, Delfino, 21, played in Italy and led Skipper Bologna to the Euroleague championship game for the 2003-04 season. Is expected to join Detroit for 2004-05 season.

Who: Andreas Glyniadakis, No. 58 pick.
Position: Center.
Ht/wt: 7-1, 280.
Team: Panellinios, Greece.
Skinny: Glyniadakis, 21, remained overseas. Expected to join the Pistons within two years.

THE REGULAR SEASON

Pistons' strategy in drafting Delfino over Brigham Young shooting guard Travis Hansen, a name frequently mentioned as a possible selection at No. 25. The Pistons didn't draft the Argentine with the idea that he would assume Jon Barry's role on the bench right away. They kept him in Europe with Italy's Skipper Bologna team for at least another year of seasoning without him counting against the salary cap.

But it's a question of quality as much as cost. The foreign players are far better fundamentally. While teenage Americans are more obsessed about proving that they've "got game," the foreigners prove that there's more value in knowing the game.

"I think we're going to be brutalized for two years because LeBron James and Carmelo Anthony, I think, are going to have an immediate impact on their teams and the league. And Darko won't play a lot."
— **Pistons coach Larry Brown**

All about Darko

According to ESPN.com, when asked what number he wants to wear, Darko told the Pistons: "Eleven."

Sorry, that was Isiah's, which has been retired.

"Thirteen?" Nope, Mehmet Okur wears that.

"Thirty-one?"

That'll work, though trainer Mike Abdenour expressed one reservation: It was worn by Mikki Moore, a 7-footer who came up short for the Pistons.

Did you know? The last two Pistons' No. 2 overall picks were Isiah Thomas (Indiana) in 1981 and Dave Bing (Syracuse) in 1966.

A wild and crazy guy: Milicic apparently has an affinity for Scores, a New York strip club. According to the New York Post, Milicic, who turned 18 in June 2003, has visited the club several times. The Post, quoting an insider, said of Darko, "He is very generous with the dancers and always buys dances for his friends, and has been known to have two girls dance for him at one time."

Brown on Darko: Interviewed on New York's WFAN radio, coach Larry Brown said: "LeBron James and Carmelo Anthony, I think, are going to have an immediate impact on their teams and the league. And Darko won't play a lot."

Darko Milicic, the No. 2 pick in the NBA draft, cut an imposing figure at media day but spent most of the season on the Pistons' bench.

THE FIRST SHIFT 14

The work begins

Former coach spoils Pistons' season opener

By Helene St. James

AUBURN HILLS (OCT. 29, 2003) — When you go to work once, you have to do it again.

The Pistons began their 2003-04 season against Indiana at the Palace by unveiling their season's slogan, which turned out to be the same one as 2002-03: "Goin' to Work."

Although the theme was not new, there were new workers to introduce.

Larry Brown ambled out to the court, stopping by the Pacers' bench to shake hands with Rick Carlisle, who was pink-slipped by the Pistons after the 2002-03 season despite working hard enough to secure two 50-victory seasons.

Carlisle got a standing ovation, and he responded with waves and a brief smile.

Fans whooped and cheered when Darko Milicic, the second overall pick in the draft, was introduced.

Tayshaun Prince got fans excited, perhaps because they're looking forward to seeing a small forward who can score. (Defense-minded Michael Curry had Prince's job in 2002-03.)

Ben Wallace and Chauncey Billups tore off the wrapping on the banner, which honored the 2002-03 Central Division title.

Billups, Richard Hamilton, Prince, Wallace and Elden Campbell started for the Pistons. That's a makeover from 2002-03, when Curry was in Prince's place and Cliff Robinson was the big man in the middle.

Right before tip-off, Wallace jogged up and hugged Carlisle.

The Pistons lost a heated battle, 89-87, and the Pistons-Pacers rivalry was alive and well.

"Do I look conflicted?" Carlisle said before the game. "It's unique. That's all I can say to you. It's odd, to say the least."

JULIAN H. GONZALEZ

Ben Wallace, left, and Chauncey Billups prepare to guide the division title banner to the Palace rafters before the season opener. Then the Indiana Pacers spoiled the party, 89-87.

Off-season deals

Pistons president of basketball operations Joe Dumars said he knew after the Nets swept the Pistons in the 2003 Eastern Conference finals that changes had to be made. Here's a list of the Pistons' off-season transactions:

May 31, 2003 — Fired coach Rick Carlisle.

June 2 — Named Larry Brown coach.

June 26 — Drafted center Darko Milicic with the No. 2 overall pick, plus two others.

July 26 — Signed free-agent center Elden Campbell to a two-year contract worth $8.4 million.

Aug. 12 — Re-signed restricted free-agent guard Richard Hamilton to a seven-year, $63-million contract.

Aug. 21 — Traded Cliff Robinson and Pepe Sanchez to Golden State for Bob Sura.

Aug. 28 — Traded small forward Michael Curry to Toronto for guard Lindsey Hunter.

Sept. 23 — Signed free-agent forward Darvin Ham to a one-year deal.

Oct. 28 — Signed free-agent forward Tremaine Fowlkes to a one-year deal.

THE REGULAR SEASON 15

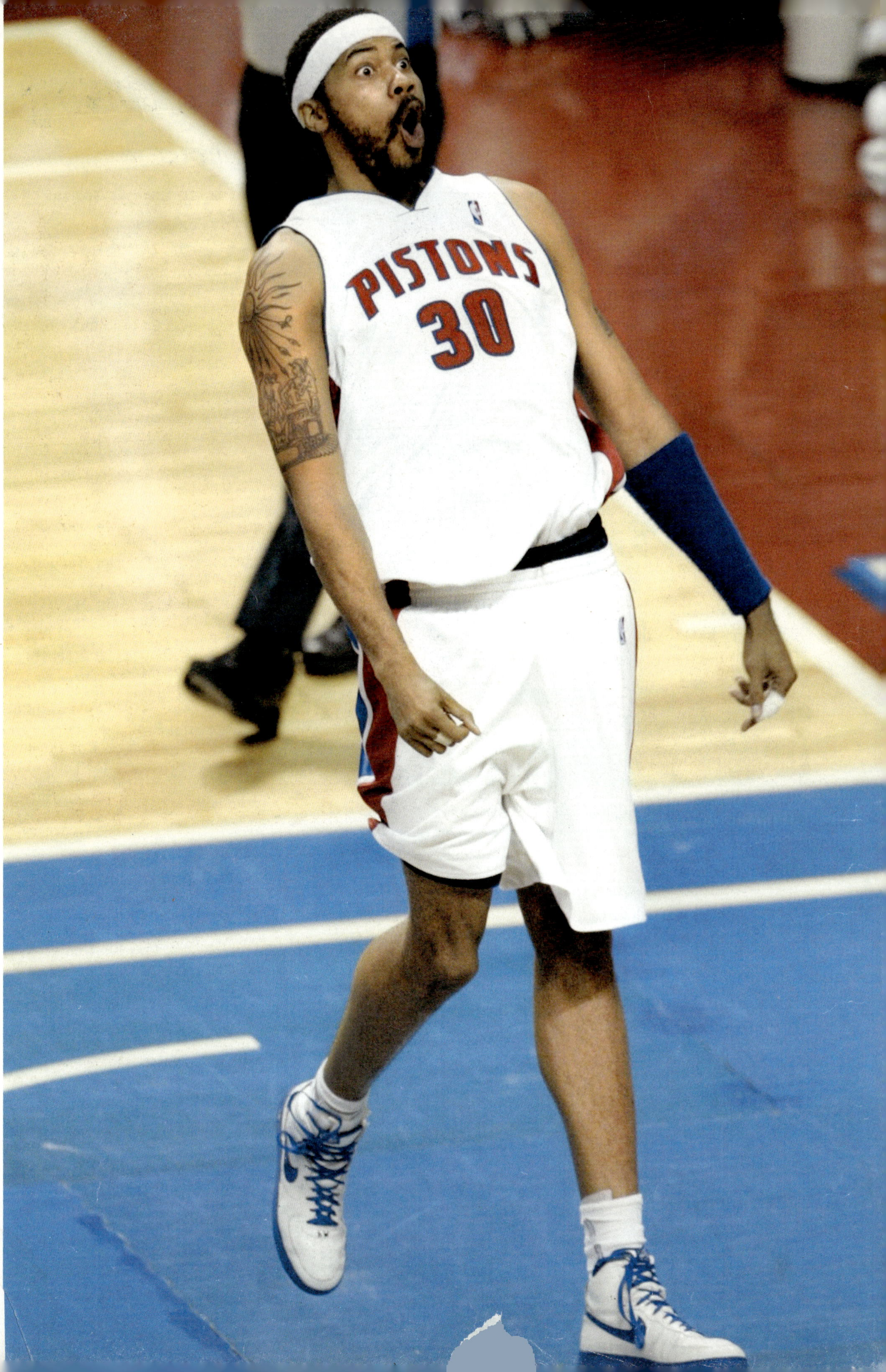
PISTONS
30

The newest bad boy

Despite Wallace's rep, Dumars makes big deal

JULIAN H. GONZALEZ

Here's a familiar scene for Rasheed Wallace: He gives it to the refs and the opposing fans give it to him.

By Mitch Albom

FEBRUARY 19, 2004 — Win. Spin. To do the former, you often need to do the latter. The wheels began turning in Detroit the moment Rasheed Wallace, a big, volatile guy whose former owner all but threw a party when he finally dumped him, joined the Pistons in a three-team trade.

So the Pistons spin. They insist he can be controlled. That environment is everything. That the new coach, Larry Brown, is a North Carolina guy like Rasheed and will have a good rapport with him. And if that's not enough, they remind you that he is, contractually, here for only a few months.

"It could be great for him, or not so great for him. It could be great for us," admitted Pistons president Joe Dumars, who gave up several mid-level players but gained an All-Star and lots of salary cap relief. "But it won't ever be bad for us. I didn't tear up my team to do this."

As for Wallace's history with marijuana, bad temper and outrageous comments?

Trade mix-up nets club fine

Rasheed Wallace's Pistons career got off to a slow start.

Wallace and Mike James, acquired in the big trade, were benched in their first game with the Pistons after the first half. It was discovered that all the paperwork from the trade had not been submitted by all parties.

The Pistons lost to Minnesota, 88-87.

The NBA fined the Pistons $200,000 as punishment for playing the two before they were eligible. The league said it was the Pistons' responsibility to make sure all details of a three-team trade were completed.

Photo on previous page by MANDI WRIGHT
A wide-eyed Rasheed Wallace skips away from an official after being called for a foul in Game 3 against the Pacers.

THE REGULAR SEASON 17

It didn't take long for the Palace fans to warm up to Rasheed Wallace, who joined the Pistons on Feb. 19 from Atlanta in a three-team deal.

"The fact is," Dumars sighed, "if you're looking for all Boy Scouts, this is the wrong league to be in."

Win. Spin. And make no mistake. This is a winning basketball move. Wallace is a major talent, a big man (6-feet-11) who can score from all over the floor. When he wants to play hard, he can change a game by himself.

Dumars believes they even need a little of Wallace's "edge," although the difference between a little and a lot of that edge is the difference between a poke in the ribs and a knife through the gut.

"What did he say to you when you spoke on the phone?" I asked Dumars.

"He was excited about coming here. He said, 'We can win this thing.'"

"And what did you say?"

"I said, 'That's what I want to hear, chief.'"

With this move, Dumars enlarges his reputation as a major front-office player. Wallace takes the Pistons from, as Dumars called it, "a pretty good team to a very, very good team."

In Portland, Wallace was part of Team Rap Sheet, a Trail Blazers group so entrenched in bad behavior it was news when players didn't get arrested.

Detroit is not a town that brooks that sort of attitude. Look around. The Red Wings are personified by quiet Steve Yzerman. Heck, Sergei Fedorov was considered a prima donna because he wanted ice time. The Lions are led by a Boy Scout quarterback, Joey Harrington. The Tigers signed Ivan (Pudge) Rodriguez because, among other things, he's considered a good guy.

But Dumars has seen that the all-good-guys thing may have a limit. The Pistons were in second place and needed a boost.

As for the players the Pistons gave up ... Bob Sura, Lindsey Hunter, Zeljko Rebraca, Chucky Atkins? None was irreplaceable. Only Atkins made a marginal difference in many games. "I hesitated on him," Dumars admitted. "But we got a good guard (Mike James) from Boston. And in the end, was I not gonna get Rasheed Wallace to keep Chucky Atkins?"

So the Pistons are no longer the quiet, blue-collar roster of the NBA.

Then again, Detroit fans have some experience in this area. Remember Bill Laimbeer? Not exactly America's Guest. But we loved him. Why? Because he wore the Pistons' uniform, that's why. They won. We spun.

The deal

The Pistons made one of their biggest trades ever in a three-team deal with Boston and Atlanta.

- The key player in the trade was forward/center Rasheed Wallace, from Atlanta, where he played one game after 7½ seasons at Portland.
- They also picked up Boston guard Mike James. They shipped backup guards Chucky Atkins and Lindsey Hunter to the Celtics and sent backup guard Bob Sura and reserve center Zeljko Rebraca to Atlanta. (The Celtics later waived Hunter, who rejoined the Pistons.) Atlanta received forward Chris Mills from Boston.
- The Pistons gave up a 2004 first-round draft pick and their rights to Milwaukee's first-round pick, which they had acquired in a previous deal.
- Dumars had to outbid former teammate Isiah Thomas for Wallace. Thomas, the New York Knicks' president, made a run at Wallace before the deadline.

WHAT THEY'RE SAYING
Comments made after the trade.

Cleveland coach Paul Silas couldn't understand why Atlanta made the deal. "That's going to make the Pistons awfully tough. I just don't know what some people are thinking about."

Thomas: "Them getting Rasheed is a great thing. I'm happy for those guys. At least now there's a couple teams over here that can challenge Indiana and New Jersey. He was a big fish on the market, and we did everything — without tearing up the core of the team — to try to get him."

L.A. Lakers guard Gary Payton: "It's going to make them the favorite in the East."

THE FIRST SHIFT 18

PISTONS' SEASON IN REVIEW

From defense to Darko

By Mark Francescutti

A look back at some of the highlights of the regular season:

BACK ON TRACK (Oct. 31, 2003) — After the season-opening loss to Indiana, Chauncey Billups and Richard Hamilton combined for 51 points in a 93-81 victory at Miami. Darko Milicic played one minute in his debut and had two turnovers and no points. Coach Larry Brown was seen giving him a stern talking-to after the game.

DREAM DAYS (Nov. 7) — Mehmet Okur had a career-high 18 rebounds in a victory over Milwaukee. "This was a dream come true. I took more rebounds than Ben Wallace," Okur said. Two nights later, Corliss Williamson scored 20 points against the Nets to help the Pistons (5-1) to their fifth straight win.

WEST COAST BLUES (Nov. 11-Nov. 15) — The Pistons went on their first West Coast trip and went 1-3. They lost close games at Sacramento, at Golden State and at Los Angeles Lakers by a combined 13 points. Detroit salvaged the trip with a victory over Phoenix, improving to 6-4.

L. EH? (Nov. 18) — The Pistons avenged the road loss to the Lakers with a 106-96 victory at the Palace. Ben Wallace took a shot on the collarbone from Shaquille O'Neal. "I don't need to apologize after what they did to me," said O'Neal, who was roughed up in the post. "(Expletive) them."

BROWN RETURNS (Nov. 26) — After five wins in six games, the Pistons played at Philadelphia, which Brown left to coach Detroit. Most of the fans booed Brown during Philly's 90-86 victory. Said Sixers star Allen Iverson: "A lot of fans probably feel betrayed. Like me, I was hurt over the whole thing, too."

JULIAN H. GONZALEZ

Milwaukee forward and former Piston Joe Smith can't get this rebound away from Mehmet Okur. Okur had one of his best games as a Piston with 12 points and 18 rebounds in a 105-99 victory on Nov. 7.

THE REGULAR SEASON   19

Mehmet Okur can only watch as Shaquille O'Neal gets an easy bucket in a Nov. 18 game at the Palace. The Pistons still won, 106-96.

JULIAN H. GONZALEZ

Before the game, Derrick Coleman, Eric Snow and Iverson hugged Brown, who said: "It was a magical night for me except for the outcome." Detroit fell to 10-6.

RIP'S BIG NIGHT (Nov. 28) — It was the kind of game a shooter like Hamilton loves. He was making shots and his teammates weren't, so he had to keep shooting. He scored a career-high 44 points in a victory over Cleveland.

DROP-OFF (Dec. 6-Dec. 12) — The Pistons looked their worst during a four-game skid to inferior competition. Yao Ming put up 22 points and 20 rebounds against Elden Campbell in a loss at Houston; the Pistons lost at home to Philadelphia, even though Iverson didn't play; they let division doormat Cleveland shoot 53 percent; they lost by 21 at home to Seattle. The only thing the fans cheered against the Sonics was Darko Milicic's baby hook shot for his first NBA basket. Detroit fell to 14-10.

CARLISLE 2, BROWN 0 (Dec. 19) — The Pacers and former coach Rick Carlisle won their second straight game over Detroit. Austin Croshere scored all 12 of his points in the fourth quarter as the Pistons squandered an 11-point lead and lost, 80-75, at Conseco Fieldhouse.

FEAR THE 'FRO (Dec. 26) — After seven losses in nine games, Wallace says he's going to become more vocal to try to help the Pistons (16-13) out of their tailspin: "Starting with me, we have to do something different."

BEN'S RESPONSE (Dec. 27) — Wallace made two free throws with 1:44 left, his first points of the game, and had a block on the next possession as the Pistons won at Atlanta, 87-84, and ended their skid.

LARRY LEAVES (Jan. 3) — On Elvis Presley impersonator night at the Palace, Elvis didn't leave the building but Brown did. Brown didn't return after officials mistakenly ejected him in the third quarter. He still earned his 900th career NBA victory, 99-93, over Golden State. Detroit set a league record by holding its 34th consecutive opponent below 100 points.

BLOND CHRISTMAS (Jan. 7) — In an 85-66 win over Houston — Detroit's seventh in a row — Darko Milicic celebrated the Serbian Orthodox Christmas with his best game and a new blond hairstyle. Milicic, who didn't score until the Pistons' 24th game, outscored Houston's Yao, 6-4, in the final 5:54. He also had four rebounds and a block.

LUCKY No. 13 (Jan. 19) — After struggling for three quarters with just four points, Billups scored 14 in the fourth, and the Pistons (29-13) tied a franchise record with their 13th straight victory, 85-77, over defending champion San Antonio. "On a scale of 1-to-10, I'd say that I'm a seven right now," Billups said when rating his growth as a Larry Brown-style point guard. Where was he a month ago? "I'd say I was a five."

CARLISLE 3, STREAK 0 (Jan. 20) — Carlisle's Pacers broke the Pistons' 13-game win streak. Tayshaun

THE FIRST SHIFT 20

STREAKY SEASON

Talk about a roller coaster. The Pistons' 2003-04 season was littered with up- and down streaks:

DATES	W-L	OVERALL
Oct. 29-Nov. 9	5-1	5-1
Nov. 11-14	0-3	5-4
Nov. 15-Dec. 3	9-2	14-6
Dec. 6-26	2-7	16-13
Dec. 27-Jan. 19	13-0	29-13
Jan. 20-25	0-3	29-16
Jan. 28-Feb. 2	4-0	33-16
Feb. 3-22	1-8	34-24
Feb. 23-March 21	12-1	46-25
March 23-25	0-2	46-27
March 27-April 12	8-1	54-28

70 AIN'T ENOUGH

The Pistons held opponents under 70 points for an NBA-record five games in a row and 11 times for the regular season:

DATE	OPPONENT	SCORE
Nov. 29	at Washington	80-69
Jan. 5	at Boston	78-68
Jan. 7	Houston	85-66
Feb. 23	at Philadelphia	76-66
March 4	at Portland	83-68
March 6	at Denver	97-66
March 7	at Seattle	86-65
March 10	Chicago	98-65
March 14	Philadelphia	85-69
April 4	Indiana	79-61
April 9	Toronto	74-66

Prince scored just two points in 27 minutes. He also violated an unwritten rule when he fouled Jermaine O'Neal and helped him up in the third quarter. Okur played just 12 minutes and didn't score. "We had two rookies in there that looked like they really didn't want to be out there," Brown said of the second-year players.

BAD CALL? (Jan. 23) — Brown was so upset that he sent assistant Mike Woodson to address the media after a 80-79 loss at Minnesota. Referee James Capers called a controversial offensive foul on Billups with two seconds left after he hit what would have been the winning shot. The officials "decided the game and not us," Billups said.

'FRO-GEDABOUDIT (Jan. 28-Feb. 2) — Wallace led the Pistons to a four-game winning streak with victories over Boston, Toronto, Memphis and Miami — all by three points or fewer and two in overtime. At Boston, Wallace went 4-for-4 from the line late to clinch a three-point victory. At Toronto, Vince Carter tried to violate the No Fly Zone in OT and was blocked by Wallace to seal a 90-89 victory. Vs. Memphis, Wallace had four blocks and four steals in an 80-78 win. At Miami, he made a game-saving block on a Lamar Odom breakaway late in regulation of a two-point overtime win. "Ben made a play I've never seen in my life," said Brown. "Amazing."

STARS ON COURT (Feb. 15) — The Western Conference won the All-Star Game, 136-132. Yao Ming started at center for the West, but Shaquille O'Neal was named MVP with 24 points and 11 rebounds off the bench. Wallace, the lone Pistons representative, had four points and seven rebounds. Chauncey Billups lost in the three-point shooting contest, and Tayshaun Prince scored 18 points in the Sophomores vs. Rookies game.

MARBURIED (Feb. 17) — The Pistons suffered their sixth-straight loss, 92-88, to New York as Stephon Marbury had 28 points. Three came on free throws with 1:08 left after referee James Capers again stifled the Pistons, calling a shooting foul on Billups, though replays indicated it was a clean block.

NEED FOR 'SHEED (Feb. 19) — The Pistons made one of their biggest trades ever, acquiring Portland's Rasheed Wallace (after a one-game stay in Atlanta). Detroit went on to lose two one-point games to Minnesota and Orlando.

DOUBLE TROUBLE (Feb. 23-March 1) — The new Wallace frontline of Ben and Rasheed began to pay dividends, with each recording a double-double in a win at Philadelphia. Detroit went on to make it four in a row before a loss at Utah. Then the fun began.

THAT UNDER 70'S SHOW (March 4-18) — The Pistons became the first team in the shot-clock era to hold three straight opponents to fewer than 70 points. They outscored Portland, Denver and Seattle, 266-199, an average of 22.3 points. The Pistons held two more opponents — Philadelphia and Chicago — under 70. The Nets broke the five-game streak by fouling to reach 70 — but the Pistons still won, 89-71, at New Jersey.

BIG WIGS (Mar. 19) — A total of 6,213 Palace fans wore Afro wigs, eclipsing the Guinness Book of World Records mark of 5,574 for people wearing wigs in a single venue. The Pistons (45-25) won the game, too, 94-75, over the Nuggets.

SWEET AND LOW (April 4) — With dual Wallaces leading the defense, the Pistons finally found a way to beat Carlisle and the Pacers for their 50th victory, 79-61. The 61 points were a season low for the Pacers and an opponent low for the Pistons. Indiana still finished the season with an NBA-best 61 wins and the top seed in the East. The Pistons won eight of their last nine to finish 54-28 under Brown (Carlisle won 50 in each of the previous two seasons as their coach). Detroit, the No. 3 seed in the East, drew Milwaukee in the first round.

Ben Wallace battles Houston's Yao Ming for a loose ball in the Pistons' 85-66 victory on Jan. 7. Yao, who scored 22 points and 22 rebounds in a Rockets' win over Detroit in December, scored just four points — two less than Darko Milicic.

JULIAN H. GONZALEZ

THE REGULAR SEASON 21

NBA SEASON IN REVIEW
From Lakers to LeBron

LAKERS DRAMA

Kobe Bryant was teary-eyed after his Lakers were ousted from the 2003 playoffs by the San Antonio Spurs? The loss ended the Lakers' run of three consecutive titles. This wasn't the last time the public saw Bryant break down. About two months later, Bryant tearfully proclaimed his innocence to the world after he was charged with sexually assaulting a 19-year-old woman in Eagle, Colo.

Unfortunately for the Lakers and the NBA, Bryant's legal troubles were the season's biggest story. The Lakers continued to grab headlines. They added future Hall of Famers Karl Malone and Gary Payton. The sniping between Shaquille O'Neal and Bryant reached a crescendo. And injuries and a reluctance to play hard consistently frustrated fans.

Through it all, the NBA's glamour team made it to the league's biggest stage before the Pistons shoved them off. But, to NBA commissioner David Stern's relief, the Lakers' melodrama didn't gobble up the entire spotlight.

LEBRON MANIA

Believe the hype.

Cleveland rookie LeBron James lifted the spirits of the Cavaliers' franchise with his dazzling play. He joined Michael Jordan and Oscar Robertson as the only players to average 20 points, five rebounds and five assists in their rookie seasons. The Cavs (35-47) didn't make the playoffs, but they were second to the Lakers as the league's biggest road draw.

James, 19, was the youngest player to win the rookie of the year award. He has emerged as a Jordan-like corporate pitchman, yet, he still flashed some "street cred." Need evidence? James showed up at a Monday Night Football game in Cleveland sporting a Jim Brown throwback jersey and a white fur coat.

Ahh, to be 19 again.

THAT OTHER ROOKIE

The 'Melo-Darko debate was argued in Detroit's barbershops, water coolers and watering holes more fiercely than war in Iraq. Did Pistons president Joe Dumars do the right thing in drafting Darko Milicic over Denver's Carmelo Anthony? The Syracuse alum didn't help Dumars' case by having a stellar season. Anthony finished second to James for rookie of the year. And unlike James, Anthony's team made the playoffs.

With each 30-point performance, Anthony is giving Dumars' detractors reason to call Milicic the next Sam Bowie. Bowie was picked ahead of Michael Jordan in 1984.

OLD FACE, SAME OL' PROBLEMS

For a guy who played less than half a season, former Michigan star Chris Webber was in the news a lot. Webber was sidelined because of a knee injury he suffered in the 2003 playoffs. His comeback was delayed after he received an eight-game suspension for lying to a federal grand jury in the Ed Martin case and violating the league's substance-abuse policy.

On the court, Webber struggled to get in sync. Kings

RICHARD LEE
Sacramento forward and former Michigan star Chris Webber walks out of a Detroit federal court in September.

2003-04 NBA STANDINGS
Eastern Conference

CENTRAL	W	L	PCT	GB	STRK	LT 10	HOME	AWAY
1z-Indiana	61	21	.744	—	W-5	8-2	34-7	27-14
3y-**Detroit**	54	28	.659	7	L-1	8-2	31-10	23-18
5y-New Orl.	41	41	.500	20	W-1	4-6	25-16	16-25
6y-Milwaukee	41	41	.500	20	L-3	5-5	27-14	14-27
Cleveland	35	47	.427	26	W-3	3-7	23-18	12-29
Toronto	33	49	.402	28	W-2	3-7	18-23	15-26
Atlanta	28	54	.341	33	L-1	5-5	18-23	10-31
Chicago	23	59	.280	38	L-2	3-7	14-27	9-32
ATLANTIC	W	L	PCT	GB	STRK	LT 10	HOME	AWAY
2x-New Jersey	47	35	.573	—	L-2	5-5	28-13	19-22
4y-Miami	42	40	.512	5	W-2	7-3	29-12	13-28
7y-New York	39	43	.476	8	L-1	6-4	23-18	16-25
8y-Boston	36	46	.439	11	W-1	4-6	19-22	17-24
Philadelphia	33	49	.402	14	L-4	3-7	21-20	12-29
Washington	25	57	.305	22	L-3	2-8	17-24	8-33
Orlando	21	61	.256	26	W-2	2-8	11-30	10-31

Western Conference

MIDWEST	W	L	PCT	GB	STRK	LT 10	HOME	AWAY
1z-Minnesota	58	24	.707	—	W-9	9-1	31-10	27-14
3y-San Ant.	57	25	.695	1	w-11	10-0	33-8	24-17
5y-Dallas	52	30	.634	6	W-2	8-2	36-5	16-25
6y-Memphis	50	32	.610	8	L-4	4-6	31-10	19-22
7y-Houston	45	37	.549	13	L-1	3-7	27-14	18-23
8y-Denver	43	39	.524	15	L-1	6-4	29-12	14-27
Utah	42	40	.512	16	L-2	5-5	28-13	14-27
PACIFIC	W	L	PCT	GB	STRK	LT 10	HOME	AWAY
2y-L.A. Lakers	56	26	.683	—	W-2	7-3	34-7	22-19
4y-Sacra.	55	27	.671	1	L-2	4-6	34-7	21-20
Portland	41	41	.500	*15	L-4	4-6	25-16	16-25
Golden State	37	45	.451	19	W-1	5-5	27-14	10-31
Seattle	37	45	.451	19	W-1	3-7	21-20	16-25
Phoenix	29	53	.354	27	W-1	5-5	18-23	11-30
L.A. Clippers	28	54	.341	28	L-1	1-9	18-23	10-31

x-division winner; y-playoff berth; z-conference title

Numerals indicate the top eight teams in each conference. The division winners and six teams from each conference with next highest number of wins total make the playoffs. In the playoffs, 1 plays 8, 2 plays 7, 3 plays 6, 4 plays 5. Teams with identical records are arranged in order of which team holds the tiebreaker advantage.

THE FIRST SHIFT 22

Cleveland's LeBron James, hailed as the next great player, lived up to the hype and won the NBA's Rookie of the Year award. Here he splits the defense of Corliss Williamson, left, and Tayshaun Prince for a bucket in a November loss to the Pistons. James ranked 13th in the NBA in scoring at 20.9 points per game.

KIRTHMON F. DOZIER

fans booed him during rough stretches. Webber's season ended when he narrowly missed a potential game-tying three-pointer in Game 7 of the West semifinals against Minnesota.

LEADER OF THE WOLF PACK

Minnesota's Kevin Garnett won the MVP award. With Sam Cassell and Latrell Sprewell playing sidekicks, the 7-foot wunderkind helped the Wolves make it out of the first round of the playoffs for the first time in franchise history. They lost to the Lakers in the Western finals.

COACHING CAROUSEL

In the year of the NBC hit reality show "The Apprentice," it seemed every coach got fired or begrudgingly resigned. The Pistons' Larry Brown, hired in June 2003, became the longest-tenured coach of the 15 teams in the East.

From the end of the 2002-03 season to the start of the Pistons-Lakers NBA Finals, 19 teams changed their coach.

At least it looks like Memphis coach Hubie Brown, 70, will be sticking around for a few years. His old-school tactics connected with the young Grizzlies, who made the their first playoff appearance in the club's nine-year history. Brown won coach of the year honors.

ISIAH TRANSFORMS KNICKS

Former Piston Isiah Thomas once scored 16 points in 94 seconds against the New York Knicks in a playoff game. As president of basketball operations for the Knicks, it seems like he turned the franchise around in a similar short amount of time.

Thomas, fired months earlier as coach of the Pacers, made numerous deals that improved the roster. One landed New York City native Stephon Marbury. Playoff basketball returned to Madison Square Garden after a two-year drought. That meant plenty of exposure for super fan Spike Lee. The fun, however, didn't last; the Knicks were swept by New Jersey.

By Al Toby

THE REGULAR SEASON

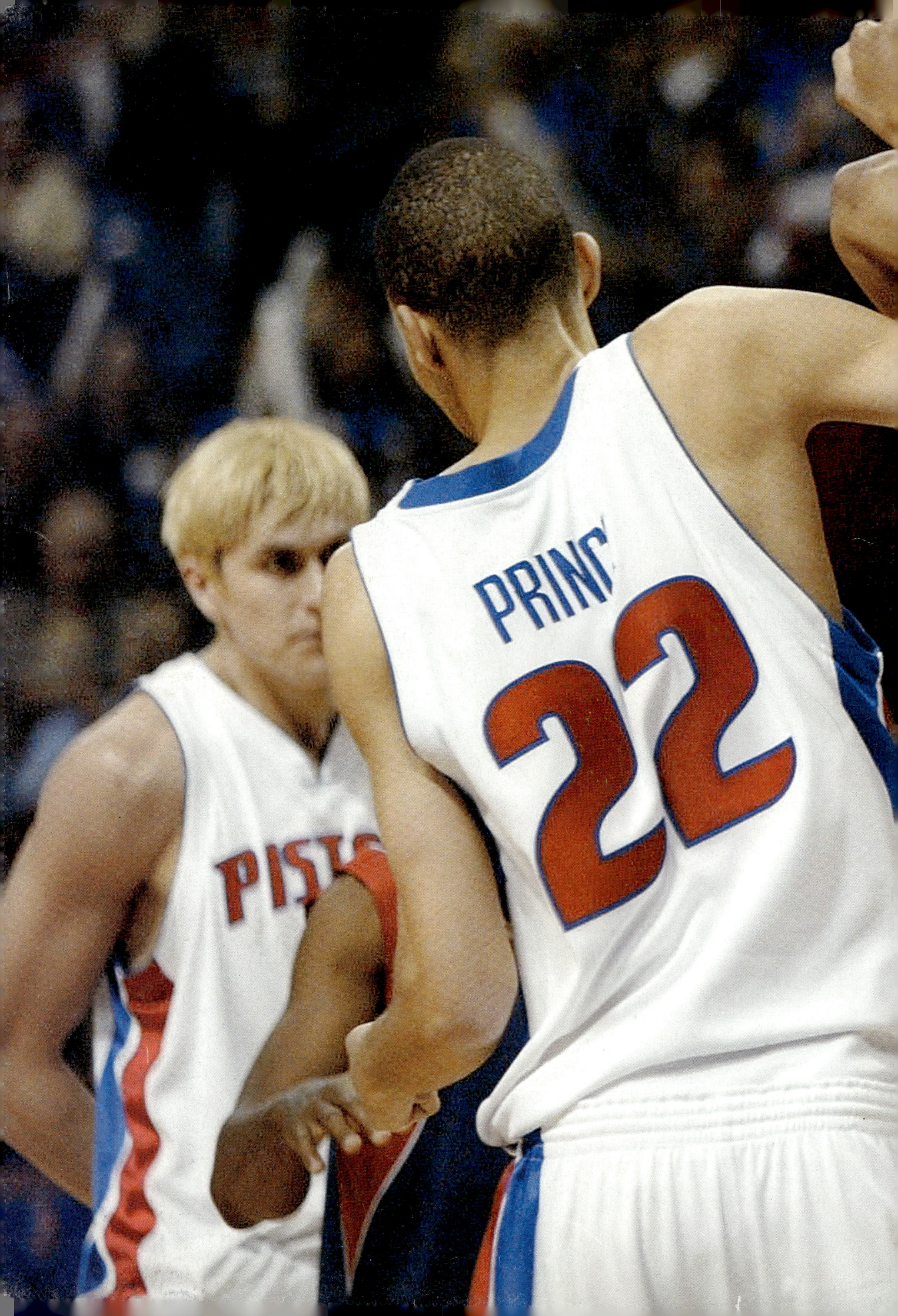
22

THE SECOND SHIFT

THE TEAM

Bridge builder

Dumars spans team's two great eras

MANDI WRIGHT

Joe Dumars, in his fourth full season as president of basketball operations, hoists the Eastern Conference championship trophy after the Pistons' Game 6 clincher against Indiana at the Palace.

By Drew Sharp

Winning breeds new friends. There was no shortage of extended hands to congratulate Joe Dumars.

But old friends give the proper context to these moments.

Standing there in the tunnel after the Pistons eliminated Indiana and advanced to the Finals, bracing herself with a cane, was Terry Daly — the First Lady of the Bad Boys.

"I'm so happy and so proud of what you've done," she said as she embraced one of "her boys" — as she often referred to Chuck Daly's players. "You've brought us back."

Winning the title for the first time in 14 years was definitely about "us." And Dumars, a Detroit guard for 14 seasons, erected the bridge between the two most significant eras in this franchise's history.

It wasn't so much that the Pistons made it back to the mountaintop, but that one of their own charted the path. Winning a title was sweeter with Dumars in charge of the team's basketball operations. He's deeply invested in the franchise's heritage, not a hired gun from the outside.

"Joe pretty much did it from scratch," said guard Chauncey Billups, one of the many complementary pieces Dumars acquired. "He didn't have much experience in the front office before taking over the job, but he had a plan of what we wanted to do."

And where he wanted to be.

"I'll be honest with you," Dumars said, "it's probably more special, more gratifying for me to get to this point for the first time as an executive than it was as a player the first time. As a player, all you have to worry about is yourself. But in my role now, you're responsible for everyone."

THE SECOND SHIFT 26

Photo on previous pages by MANDI WRIGHT

The Pistons brought back the team concept to the NBA, as demonstrated by the bonding of Tayshaun Prince and Darvin Ham.

Guard Lindsey Hunter — one of the most veteran Pistons — shares a laugh with one of his former teammates, Joe Dumars.

KIRTHMON F. DOZIER

There's vindication. Those who questioned the rationale of kicking Rick Carlisle to the curb and offering Larry Brown $30 million for five years must forever hold their silence. And Dumars' reasoning for selecting Darko Milicic with the second pick in the 2003 draft was justified. Dumars could afford zero contributions from such a high selection.

He might have been the only one who envisioned this day when he took over on June 6, 2000. It wasn't the smoothest of transitions. Dumars had little choice but to bring back interim coach George Irvine. He was poorly prepared for the draft three weeks later, resulting in the selection of Michigan State's Mateen Cleaves with a first-round pick.

"I remember speaking with Mr. D," Dumars said of owner Bill Davidson. "I looked him right in the eye and told him that this wasn't going to take forever. I wasn't going to con him with any of these five-year or seven-year plans that people try to sell everyone."

Dumars — who won NBA executive of the year in his second full season — gave the franchise street cred in the player network. He promised a quick recovery, but that required two components rarely seen in sports executives these days — a willingness to take risks and quickly cut losses.

He turned Grant Hill into Ben Wallace and Jerry Stackhouse into Rip Hamilton.

Dumars reigns over a roster that is unique in the NBA. He did not follow the get-one-superstar-and-surround-him-with-affordable-role-players model. Oh, they told him he should.

They told him that's what works. But he said no thanks. Using his knowledge of players he had bumped against, he built around defense.

"We have a team that is hungry at every position," he says, "because nearly all of them were told at some point that they weren't good enough. Ben Wallace wasn't even drafted. Chauncey Billups has bounced around four or five teams. Rasheed (Wallace) was supposed to be too much trouble. Rip wasn't good enough to hold onto. Tayshaun (Prince) fell down to late in the first round on draft day.

"They are united by the idea that someone doubted them. That's a good spirit to bring together."

Playoff progress

After failing to make the playoffs in 2001, the Pistons are on a three-year run in which they have advanced one round further each season:

2002
East quarterfinals:
Beat Toronto, 3-2
East semifinals:
Lost to Boston, 4-1

2003
East quarterfinals:
Beat Orlando, 4-3
East semifinals:
Beat Philadelphia, 4-2
East finals:
Lost to New Jersey, 4-0

2004
East quarterfinals:
Beat Milwaukee, 4-1
East semifinals:
Beat New Jersey, 4-3
East finals: Beat Indiana, 4-2
NBA Finals: Beat L.A. Lakers.

THE TEAM 27

Brown's sacrifice
Legendary coach gave up family time for title

Larry Brown makes a point during the Pistons' Game 5 victory at the Palace, the first-round clincher against Milwaukee.

ERIC SEALS

By Jemele Hill

They ate dinner together three or four times a week; afterward, they played cards or charades.

But cards were hard when it was just the three of them. And charades just weren't as funny without Dad.

This was the quiet sacrifice Larry Brown made when he came to Detroit, the one not publicized. The Pistons gave him a handsome contract — five years for about $30 million — but his family has paid a price for Brown to win his first title.

Brown, 63, spent the season apart from his wife and two young children. While he was the Pistons' coach this season, he also was a father missed by his wife, Shelly, his 7-year-old daughter, Madison, and 9-year-old son, L.J.

They stayed in Philadelphia, where Brown coached the 76ers for six seasons before coming to Detroit in June.

"It's terrible," he said of the separation. "This has been the worst year in terms of family. Thank God for airplanes. My kids think the apartment I live in is a hotel. They asked for room service the other night. It's not a comfortable situation, but we're going to correct it."

The Browns, including their two 100-pound Labrador retrievers, intended to move to their recently purchased home in West Bloomfield once the kids finished the school year.

Brown — who also has three adult daughters, Kristen, Alli and Melissa — has coached seven NBA teams, but none of those moves was like this one. During the regular season, he would fly to Philadelphia one week and his family would come the next to Birmingham, where he rented a condominium.

"My kid said I should go back and get a job in Philly," Brown said of L.J.

Brown was as involved a parent as he could be, but it still was hard for him not to feel as if he were missing out. Madison began ice skating, and he missed some of her performances. During the winter, Shelly had her hands full when both kids had the flu.

"I was thinking, 'I could use an extra pair of hands,'" she said, laughing.

Instead, Brown had to settle for detailed accounts of what's going

THE SECOND SHIFT 28

on at home. It wasn't ideal, but the children began to somewhat enjoy telling their father stories about their lives.

"It's always a good laugh at the end of the week to bring up things they said or did," Shelly said, "even if they have to share it with him on Tuesday instead of when it happened on Friday. I think they get a kick out of telling him all of their fun stuff."

Besides, his family is somewhat used to this lifestyle. The coaching profession is not kind to families, and Brown's has become accustomed to his absences.

When the Pistons hired Brown last June, he and his wife considered moving everyone to the Detroit area at the same time. But they didn't want to pull their children out of school.

Plus, it gave Shelly Brown an opportunity she didn't have when her husband went to the Indiana Pacers in 1993. She had to coordinate that move when she was pregnant with L.J., and it happened so suddenly she didn't have time to investigate anything. This time, she had months to research neighborhoods and schools.

"The kids were involved in choosing their school," Shelly said. "Everybody was on board and kind of excited. They got to finish the school year. It's a lot easier in hindsight."

While it's a sacrifice now, the Browns soon will have a lot of time to spend together. They are traveling to Athens, where Larry will coach the U.S. Olympic team in August.

"Even though it was a long season for all of us," Shelly said, "it's all going to work out for the best."

A man for all seasons

After victories at the Palace, Larry Brown showed his hometown spirit. He donned a Pudge Rodriguez jersey (top left), a Steve Yzerman jersey (top right) and a Charles Rogers jersey (bottom right).

After Tampa Bay won the Stanley Cup, Brown wore a Lightning jersey to honor Pistons and Lightning owner Bill Davidson.

What else is out there? Maybe a Shock jersey or a Fury jersey? How about the retro look?

He could find some dandies from his coaching past: Carolina Cougars (Billy Cunningham,1973), Denver Nuggets (Dan Issel, 1978) and Kansas Jayhawks (Danny Manning, 1988).

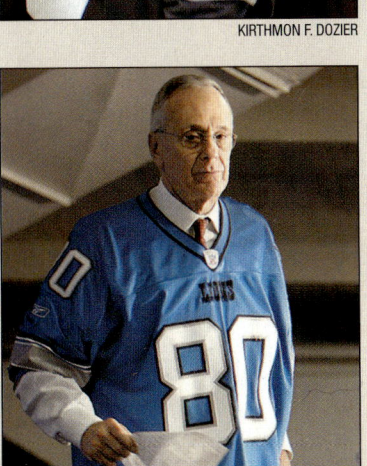

THE BROWN FILE

Age: 63 (born Sept. 14, 1940, Brooklyn, N.Y.).

High school: Long Beach High (Long Beach, N.Y.), graduated 1959.

College: University of North Carolina, graduated 1963 . . . All-ACC, 1963 . . . Led team in scoring as a junior with 16.5 points . . . Member of gold medal-winning U.S. Olympic team, 1964.

Pro career: Played for five ABA teams: New Orleans Buccaneers, 1967-68; Oakland Oaks, 1968-69; Washington Capitols, 1969-70; Virginia Squires, 1970-71; Denver Rockets, 1971-72 . . . ABA All-Star three times, 1968-70; All-Star MVP, 1968 . . . Member of ABA championship team with Oakland, 1969.

Coaching highlights: NBA — 879-685 in 20 seasons, 69-72 in 15 playoff bids, coach of the year with 76ers in 2001. . . ABA — 229-107 in four seasons, 20-22 in four playoff bids, coach of the year, 1973, 1975, 1976 . . . College — 177-61 in seven seasons, won NCAA championship and coach of the year in 1988 at Kansas . . . Inducted into Hall of Fame, Sept. 27, 2002.

Family: Wife, Shelly; children, L. J., Madison, Kristen, Alli and Melissa. . . His brother, assistant coach Herb Brown, was head coach of Pistons in 1978 . . . Larry Brown is 5-9, 160 pounds.

MAN ON THE MOVE

Brown's coaching career (records include ABA and NBA playoffs):

TEAM	YEARS	RECORD
Carolina Cougars (ABA)	1972-74	111-73
Denver Rockets/ Nuggets (ABA)	1974-76	138-56
Denver Nuggets (NBA)	1976-79	134-102
UCLA	1979-81	42-17
New Jersey Nets (NBA)	1981-83	91-69
University of Kansas	1983-88	135-44
San Antonio Spurs (NBA)	1988-91	160-138
Los Angeles Clippers (NBA)	1991-93	68-59
Indiana Pacers (NBA)	1994-97	212-154
Philadelphia 76ers (NBA)	1998-03	283-235

Assistants: Herb Brown (Vermont '57); Dave Hanners (North Carolina '76); Igor Kokoskov (Belgrade University '93); John Kuester (North Carolina '77); Mike Woodson (Indiana '80).

Athletic trainer: Mike Abdenour.

Strength and conditioning coach: Arnie Kander.

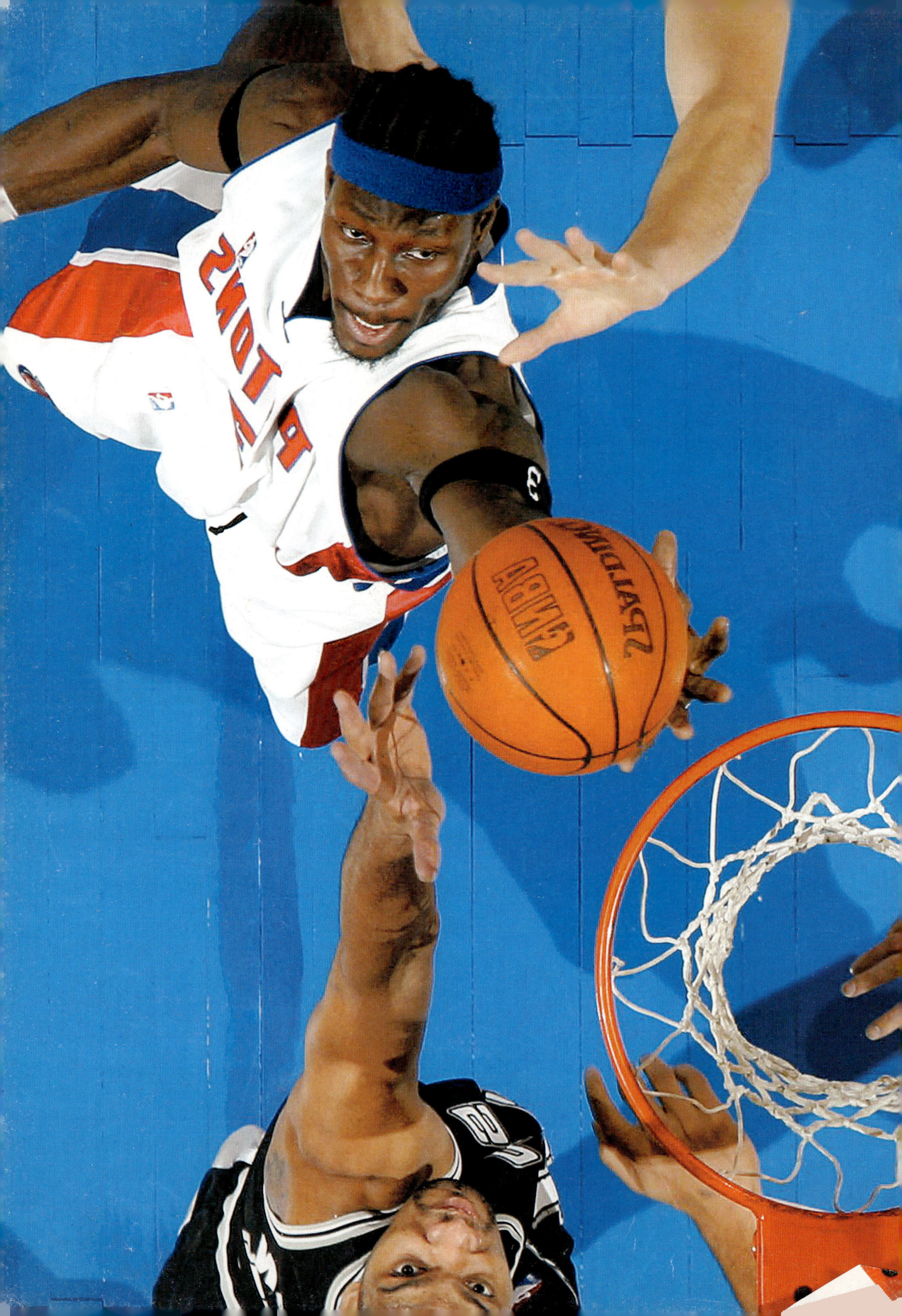
PISTONS

Seven to star

Seven moments shape Ben Wallace's career

Ben Wallace became more of a vocal leader in the locker room and an offensive threat on the court.

By Mitch Albom

When we begin this story, Ben Wallace is just a teenager. A poor kid from a huge family, he has saved the money he has earned from picking pecans and cutting hair in his small town of White Hall, Ala., and he has paid to attend a basketball camp hosted by Charles Oakley of the New York Knicks. There are rambunctious, big-dreaming kids — and they're making noise and their attention span is short. And Oakley, who is trying to talk, is exasperated.

Finally he bellows, "OK, if y'all think you know it all, who's gonna step up and play me one-on-one?"

Wallace, who was quiet the whole time, looks around. And then someone points at him and yells, "He'll play you!"

"She was the person I always knew I could turn to, the one person who would ask no questions ..."
— Pistons forward Ben Wallace speaking about his mother, Sadie Wallace, who died in 2003.

Huh? Wallace swallows. Oakley glares. "Come on then," says this pro athlete nearly 11 years his senior. One of Ben's older brothers walks in, sizes up the situation and nods. "Go on and play him," he says. Ben takes the ball at Oakley, an NBA tough guy.

And Ben bloodies his lip. And Oakley bloodies Ben's lip, too.

Later, Oakley says, "Now, if you play like that all the time, maybe you'll have a chance." And he gives him his phone number.

How did Ben Wallace become the league's best defensive player for two straight years, a towering force on the Pistons?

The Oakley saga was one defining moment. Here are six more.

Second moment. He is a high school senior, a 6-foot-7 football star. But basketball is in his heart. He visits Auburn because coaches say he "can play both."

Spying guys playing hoops, Ben tells his recruiting coach, "I think I can take those guys."

"What are you talking about?" the coach says.

"When I play basketball here. I can take those guys if they're on

Photo on previous page by JULIAN H. GONZALEZ
The bigger they are ... Ben Wallace snatches a rebound before San Antonio star Tim Duncan can get a hand on it.

the team."

The coach clarifies it: "You can play both ways. Offense and defense. But not basketball."

Wallace comes home, finds an old phone number and dials it.

"So, you ready to play basketball?" says Oakley. "If you are, I know a guy who's coaching junior college in Ohio. ..."

Third moment. Sophomore year at college. Wallace, raised as the second-youngest of 11 children by his single mother, Sadie, comes home with a sudden desire: He wants to contact his birth father, who he has seen a few times.

"Why?" he is asked now.

"I guess because I was becoming a man myself," he answers. "I was thinking about what I'd be like as a father. And I wanted to know his side of the story."

When the man shows up — his name is Samuel Doss — he begins to explain himself.

"And then he called me 'Son,'" Ben says, his voice dropping. "I got a little ticked off. I told him, 'My name is Ben. You don't have the right to call me Son.'"

The man apologizes; the conversation continues. The man tells Ben he has 20 children, that he has "gotten in over his head," that he can't do the things he wants to do. His time and funds are limited.

Money wasn't the issue. "It was just, "'Why couldn't you come around some time? ...'"

His dad dies three years later.

Fourth moment. The 1996 NBA draft. Wallace, who has transferred to Division II Virginia Union — the school Oakley attended — has blossomed into a solid player. Several teams tell him they plan to draft him in the second (and final) round.

He watches the draft. His name is never called. He swallows hard, goes to the gym and works on his game the rest of the night.

Fifth moment. The Boston Celtics have invited him to a summer league. He plays well, but they keep using him as a small forward, running around on the perimeter. He wants to play inside. But he doesn't complain.

The summer ends. The Celtics say they'll call him.

Finally, a phone call comes, but it's an Italian team.

With no other prospects, he gets a passport.

Sixth moment. He is in Calabria, Italy, in the mountains between two seas and a short hop from the shores of Sicily.

He plays a few weeks in Italy. Then another call. It's his agent, telling him Washington wants to give him a tryout. He doesn't want to play small forward. In his mind, he's a center or power forward. In Italy, they use him that way.

He calls back and says "No."

The next day, he is still in Italy, figuring, that's that. Who knows?

And the phone rings again. This time it's Wes Unseld, the Washington general manager. And he says, "Son, I want to assure you we're looking for a power forward and a center."

Ben comes home.

Seventh moment. He is in the NBA with Detroit. He has improved every year. As the reigning NBA defensive player of the year, Big Ben is admired by teammates, coaches and fans alike, a strong, silent celebrity.

It is halftime of a game against New Jersey. Wallace has tied a franchise record with seven blocks. This is what he does. He blocks. He rebounds. He changes the game. He is 28, one week away from his first All-Star Game.

And then president Joe Dumars pulls him aside.

"It's your mother," Dumars says. "She's in the hospital. ..."

By the time Wallace lands in Alabama, she is gone.

The days that follow are a patched quilt of emotions: grief, love, obligation, strength, memory, pride, heartbreak.

And, finally, acceptance.

"She was the person I always knew I could turn to, the one person who would ask no questions — it'd just be like, 'It's all right, it's all right.' If I felt, at times, that I couldn't stick it out, she'd be like, 'Come home, just come home, you can always come home.'"

Now home had changed.

So he changed, too.

Think about where Wallace — now 29, married, a father of three, wealthy, popular and successful — might be if any of these moments had gone a different way.

BEN WALLACE

Position: Forward/center.
Age: 29.
Born: Sept. 10, 1974, White Hall, Ala.
Height: 6-feet-9.
Weight: 240 pounds.
Drafted: Never drafted.
College: Virginia Union.
NBA experience: 8 years.
How acquired: Traded from Orlando with Chucky Atkins to Detroit for Grant Hill in 2000.

STATISTICS

REGULAR SEASON

G	MIN	REB	AST	PTS
81	37.7	12.4	1.7	9.5

CAREER

G	MIN	REB	AST	PTS
542	29.7	10.4	1.1	6.1

NOTABLE

■ A fan favorite because of his inspiring and intimidating defensive play and his larger-than-life Afro, Big Ben finished second to Indiana's Ron Artest in voting for NBA defensive player of the year.

■ Named to All-NBA second team for second straight season and NBA all-defensive first team for third straight season.

■ Ranked second in NBA in rebounds (12.4) and blocked shots (3.0) during regular season.

■ Was named to 2004 Athens U.S. Olympic team.

JULIAN H. GONZALEZ

For all the talent that's come together for the Pistons this season, Big Ben still gives the team its center, its grit.

THE SECOND SHIFT

The real Rasheed
Who is he really? You decide

Earned or not, Rasheed Wallace had a bad rep for his temper when he was in Portland. But he has been a good fit for the Pistons.

This story contains a quote with a racial epithet that the Free Press considers obscene and generally does not publish. We decided to include the word because it showed why the quote was so controversial.

"Everybody is not going to like you. ... You just gotta keep walking that straight path."
— Pistons forward/center Rasheed Wallace

By Michael Rosenberg

In a meaningless regular-season game against Toronto, Pistons forward Rasheed Wallace received his 197th career technical foul. Minutes later, he was still complaining to the officials, and he almost got No. 198.

At halftime, he went out of his way to play with teammate Darvin Ham's children — laughing, smiling, doing a magic trick. In the second half, Wallace took three shots and didn't make any. But his team won, so he was happy.

The Pistons entered the playoffs with their best championship hopes in more than a decade. Those hopes hinged largely on Wallace, the team's most talented player, who will be a free agent after the season and might be gone in July.

Who is Rasheed Wallace?

He has been known to spend hours at a time reading to kids, and also to blow past fans and well-wishers without acknowledging them.

He doesn't like attention, but in a rare interview in December, he unleashed some controversial comments.

He constantly battles officials, but he never criticizes teammates. He is the fourth-highest-paid player in the NBA, but loves to practice with the second team. He is a doting father, husband and son, but he prefers to talk only about basketball.

"It's awfully hard to describe him," said Bill Schonely, the longtime announcer for the Portland Trail Blazers, Wallace's team for 7½ seasons. "He could turn on the charm when he wanted to, but he didn't do it too often. He just turned everybody off. I've been around athletes all my life, and I just hate that. He was a blight on the organization. They almost had a parade downtown when they made that deal."

Rasheed Wallace: "Simple fact: The people who are criticizing me don't know me."

When the Pistons traded for Wallace in February, they added one of the league's most volatile players to its most businesslike team. Would it work?

Wallace's scoring average was his lowest since he was a rookie, but this seems to be the happiest time of his NBA career. When Wallace missed games because of injuries after joining the Pistons, he sat on the bench in full uniform, instead of the usual street clothes, and cheered his teammates.

In Portland, he was considered the most incorrigible player on the league's most insufferable team. In Detroit, he is considered the most important cog on one of the league's most likable teams.

"He's like a chameleon," Ham said. "He blends in with his environment."

◆ ◆ ◆

Rasheed Abdul Wallace was only in ninth grade, but he had serious talent. Even then, you could tell he might be one of the best to come through Simon Gratz High in Philadelphia.

"Absolutely," Martin Clair said. "It was a pleasure to have the kid in art class. He was as good as anybody. He was artistic."

Not just artistic — passionate about art. Wallace filled notebooks with drawings. If he didn't play pro basketball, Wallace said he would almost certainly have pursued "something in that art field."

But it was clear — even in high school — that Wallace would play pro basketball.

Wallace was such a hoops talent that North Carolina coach Dean Smith, who holds the record for all-time victories in college basketball, made a recruiting visit to Philly as soon as his team ended its season.

Wallace was named USA Today's national player of the year.

But he didn't lead the team in scoring. A kid named Rondell Turner scored more. Wallace refused to shoot if somebody else had a better shot — and, because Wallace always was double-teamed, somebody else almost always had a better shot. When Simon Gratz built a big lead, Wallace would turn to coach Bill Ellerbee and ask to come out of the game, so the backups could play.

Hang on to this portrait of the artist as a young man. Remember it when the chameleon changes environments.

Wallace's friends from Philly and North Carolina heard about this serial boor, this plague upon the league, and they were stunned.

Rasheed Wallace? Serial boor? Huh?

"So many times that would pass through my mind," said Pat Sullivan, who played with Wallace at North Carolina and is a Pistons assistant coach. "It would bother me a lot. I knew, deep down, that's not the guy I know."

From most public evidence, it was the guy he had become. He set an NBA record with 41 technical fouls in one season — breaking his own record from the previous year.

Wallace got so angry with the media that he wouldn't talk to the Trail Blazers' broadcasters, who are employed by the team.

The Blazers stockpiled players of questionable character (they earned the nickname "Jail Blazers"), and Wallace, the team's best player, was called the biggest

JULIAN H. GONZALEZ

Rasheed Wallace drives the lane against Indiana's Jermaine O'Neal during Game 4 of the Eastern Conference finals. Wallace and O'Neal were teammates in Portland for four years.

THE SECOND SHIFT 34

problem.

He still had a loyal following. The hip-hop generation always has loved 'Sheed. But among old-school fans, Wallace had one of the worst reputations in the league. The mere mention of his name caused a visceral reaction.

Fans saw this big, angry, black dude, with a huge tattoo from right elbow to right shoulder, and a snarling bulldog tattoo on his left biceps, flashing his temper on the court.

In this environment, the chameleon couldn't witness a bad call without snapping at the officials.

"I'm not like a whole bunch of these young boys out here and get captivated into the league," Wallace told the Oregonian in December. "No. I see behind the lines. I see behind the false screens. . . . In my opinion, they just want to draft niggers who are dumb and dumber — straight out of high school."

The critics were appalled, but not shocked.

"By the time that article came out, that didn't surprise me one bit," said Schonely. "That was typical Rasheed."

In a statement released through the Trail Blazers, Wallace apologized for the "street language" but not for the message. The apology was dismissed, but think about it for a second. Many young black men use the n-word freely, and that's why Wallace used it. Without the street language, would Wallace's comments have caused such a stir?

"It's part of everyday vernacular for me," said Wallace, 29. "Some people were upset by what I said, and some weren't. But there again: If it's on my mind, I'm going to say it. I ain't scared to say what I'm thinking."

This much is clear: Rasheed Wallace and the city of Portland were deep into a dysfunctional relationship, and he was ill-equipped to dig himself out.

He wouldn't even try.

"There were always enough times for autographs, and he'd just blow them off," Schonely said. "He was just blatant about it. 'Get away from me! I'm not signing anything!' You can't sign 'em all, but you could sign some."

Once, the team asked him to distribute Christmas trees to needy families. According to Sports Illustrated, he spent the whole time on his cell phone and checking his pager. Another time, he and teammate Damon Stoudamire were arrested for having marijuana in their car. This was Portland's picture of Rasheed Wallace: biggest hoodlum on a team of hoodlums — the chameleon had become his environment.

But wait. Change the environment, just a bit, and . . .

"Too many people don't know that Rasheed is in many ways an outstanding individual," said John Nash, the Blazers general manager who traded Wallace.

"He was very cooperative in community affairs. He would be the cheerleader of the Read to Achieve program. He loved visiting the Head Start program. He didn't just show up. He was emotionally involved in it."

Wallace's environment changed again in February, when he was traded — first to Atlanta, for one game, and then to Detroit. With the Pistons, Wallace has found his most comfortable environment in the NBA.

He fits the room.

And yet, the more he tries to blend in, the more he stands out.

"Everybody is not going to like you," Wallace said. "Everybody is not going to like what you do. Fifty percent like you, 50 percent hate you. You just gotta keep walking that straight path."

Rasheed Wallace pleads his case to official Joe DeRosa after being tagged with a foul in Game 2 against the Pacers.

ROMAIN BLANQUART

RASHEED WALLACE

Position: Forward/center.
Age: 29.
Born: Sept. 17, 1974, Philadelphia.
Height: 6-feet-11.
Weight: 230 pounds.
Drafted: First round (fourth overall) by Washington in 1995.
College: North Carolina.
NBA experience: 9 years.
How acquired: From Atlanta in a three-team trade in February.

STATISTICS

REGULAR SEASON
G	MIN	REB	AST	PTS
68	35.1	6.8	2.3	16.0

CAREER
G	MIN	REB	AST	PTS
632	34.5	6.7	1.9	16.0

NOTABLE

■ Widely regarded as the final piece to the championship puzzle when he was acquired at the trade deadline. 'Sheed solidified the best defense in the NBA.

■ On a team of distinctive hairstyles, Rasheed's signature is a patch of white hair and a headband.

■ After his rookie season in Washington, he spent seven-plus seasons in Portland before getting shipped to Atlanta, where he played one game before the trade.

■ Struggled with plantar fasciitis in his left foot in the early part of the playoffs. The ailment is an inflammation caused by excessive stretching of the plantar fascia, a thick band of tissue that covers the bones on the bottom of the foot. Wallace described it saying it was like a rock was in his shoe.

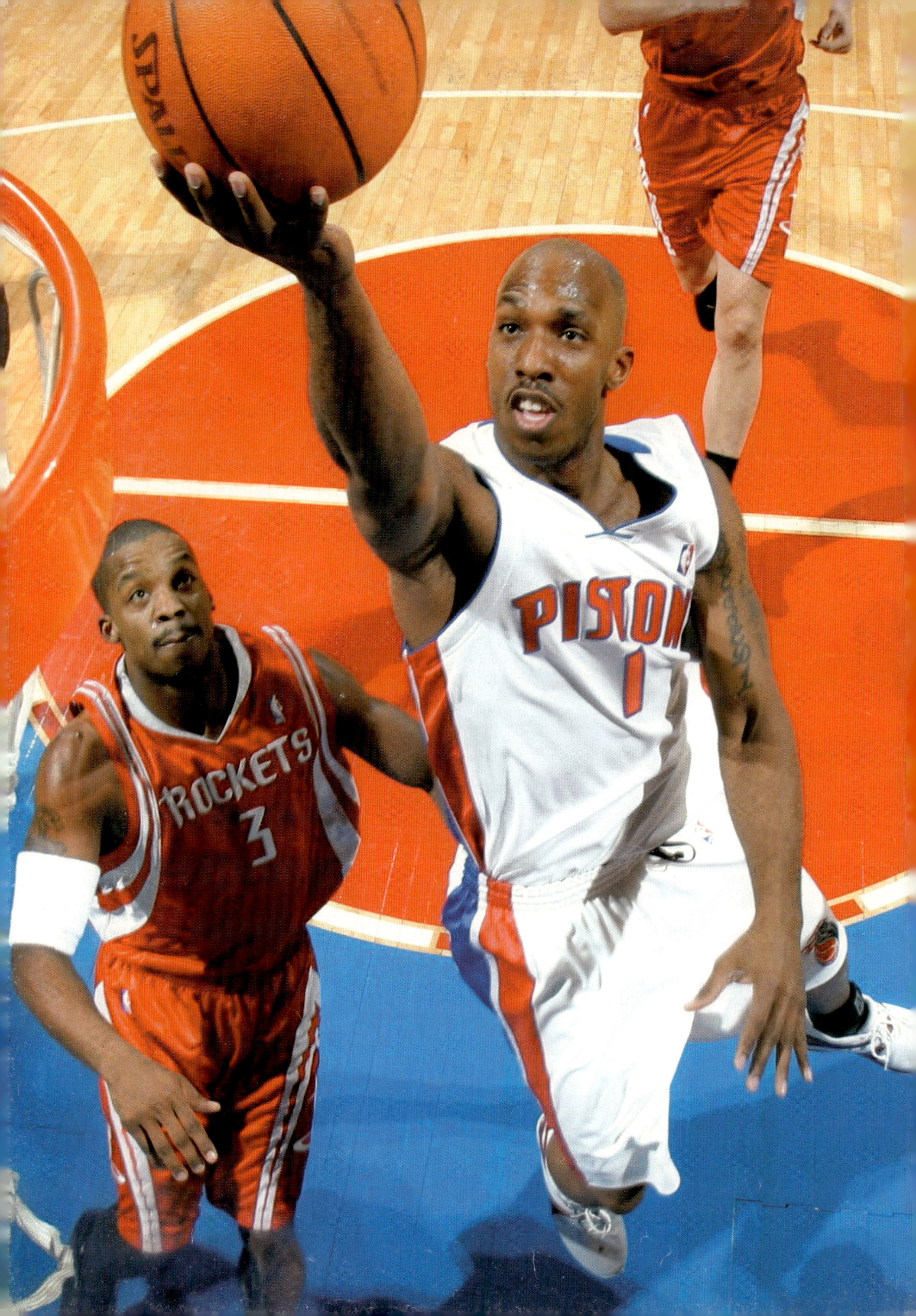
PISTONS
1
ROCKETS
3

Getting the point

Billups adjusts his game to life in Brown's town

Chauncey Billups has become a team leader and made his game more well-rounded.

By Drew Sharp and Perry A. Farrell

It only seems that Chauncey Billups has been in the NBA forever.

"I was talking to somebody about that a little while ago," Billups said, laughing. "I've been in the league now seven years. I've played for six teams and for eight different head coaches. That's more than a career's worth of change for most. It could make you crazy if you let it."

He's only 27, yet Billups bears the marks of the long, grinding playoff road, a path that's only fulfilled for one team. A crushing barrier awaits everybody else.

"You keep hitting that wall enough, you do one of two things," he said. "Either you back down because it hurts too much, or you go back at it even harder to knock your way through it."

It is one of the few areas where stubbornness is a virtue. There is no compromise.

Had Billups taken a similar approach in his occasionally bumpy relationship with Head Coach No. 8, Larry Brown, the Pistons wouldn't be in the position they're in today.

"There had to be some mutual sacrifice for this to work out," Billups said. "There was a lot of

"There was a lot of give-and-take. I listened to Coach Brown because he knows the game and he's going to make me a better player.

— **Pistons guard Chauncey Billups**

give-and-take. I listened to Coach Brown because he knows the game and he's going to make me a better player. But he had a certain idea of what he thought a point guard should be, but I knew what my strengths were as a shooting guard so we had to mix in a little of this with a little of that."

And the finished product was the hybrid that has become customary in the NBA.

It's not about having the best point guard, but the best lead guard.

"It's a new game," Billups said. "I

Photo on previous page by JULIAN H. GONZALEZ
Chauncey Billups, here gliding past Houston's Steve Francis for a lay-up, had to change his playing style under Larry Brown.

Chauncey Billups couldn't wait to pick up his Bentley Continental GT. "It's classy, but it's sporty," he said. "And it's real comfortable, plenty of room."

PATRICIA BECK

Driving with Chauncey

Question: Why did you pick a Bentley Continental GT, instead of a Rolls-Royce or something else?

Answer: I always wanted a Bentley.

Q: Did you have any special modifications, anything added?

A: No. I just wanted to get it. I didn't want to wait anymore.

Q: How long have you been waiting for this car?

A: About a year and a half.

Q: Did you pick the color, silver with black interior?

A: Yeah. All my cars are silver, because it looks good with chrome wheels. It's a perfect match.

Q: What about during the winter?

A: I've got a Range Rover for that. This'll just be for the summertime and some nice days.

Q: What was your first car?

A: An Olds 98. I don't even remember what year it was. It was about as long as this building. I'd only drive about three days a week, because it cost so much to fill up.

Q: What do you like about the Continental GT?

A: It's classy, but it's sporty. And it's real comfortable, plenty of room.

Q: What do you want your license plate to say?

A: BIG SHOT. They call me Mr. Big Shot, but I don't know if I can get that many letters.

By Jamie Butters

CHAUNCEY BILLUPS

Position: Guard.
Age: 27.
Born: Sept. 25, 1976, Denver.
Height: 6-feet-3.
Weight: 202 pounds.
Drafted: First round (third overall) by Boston in 1997.
College: Colorado.
NBA experience: 7 years.
How acquired: Signed as a free agent in 2002.

STATISTICS

REGULAR SEASON

G	MIN	REB	AST	PTS
78	35.4	3.5	5.7	16.9

CAREER

G	MIN	REB	AST	PTS
449	29.5	2.8	4.4	13.1

NOTABLE

■ Appropriately dubbed Mr. Big Shot by broadcaster George Blaha, because Billups has a knack for sinking clutch shots, such as the half-courter he sank to force overtime in Game 5 of the New Jersey series.

■ Co-captain and friend to numerous young players, including Tayshaun Prince and Darko Milicic.

■ Set regular-season career highs in minutes (35.4), points (16.9) and assists (5.7).

■ Named Mr. Basketball in Colorado three times while in high school, he was a McDonald's All-America as a senior.

---

know Coach doesn't like hearing that. He's so old-school. But the days of having a John Stockton-type of point guard running your team are over. ... The better guards have to be able to do everything — distribute, score and run the offense."

However, the defining moment in their relationship may have come March 6, and it has been smooth sailing — as smooth as it could get with Brown — as the Pistons rode a five-game winning streak, allowing fewer than 70 points per game.

That date was when the Pistons were in Billups' hometown of Denver and he took just five shots while handing out 13 assists as Detroit destroyed the Nuggets, 91-66. Brown hailed Billups' play that night as one of the team's most unselfish acts of the season.

After an 85-69 victory over Philadelphia on March 14, Brown was still praising his point guard, who scored just 13 points but had nine assists while taking just eight shots.

"I don't think I've seen Chauncey play this good all-around all season," Brown said. "That has been a huge key to this team on both ends because he's trying to give it up, and he does things that we've been asking him to do all year."

For the season, he averaged 16.9 points, 3.5 rebounds and 5.7 assists.

"I've done a better job of knowing what Larry likes and knowing how I can do that and do what I like to do," Billups said.

The playoffs are about guard play.

It's why the Pistons' fate in the playoffs was directly tied to Billups' performance.

"It's been tremendous working with Chauncey this season," Brown said. "I always respected him as a player before I got here, and after working with him for a year, I discovered that he's even better than I thought."

The Pistons are Billups' team. He's not as vocal as Rasheed Wallace or as menacing as Ben Wallace, but he remains the only player we know who isn't afraid to take the big shot late in a big game.

Billups has been around long enough to know there aren't endless opportunities. He's the point man for a team molded to have the best of both worlds — good enough to compete for a championship today, while still youthful enough to challenge three or four years later.

For someone who has been uprooted his entire career, Billups is firmly grounded.

THE SECOND SHIFT 38

Get shorty

Energizer bunny Hamilton excels at a job nobody else wanted

Rip Hamilton displays an easygoing smile as he faces the media without his trademark mask, which he wore to protect a broken nose.

By Mitch Albom

"The good thing when you pull up to shoot is that nobody knows where you're gonna do it but you."
— **Pistons guard Richard Hamilton**

It is a story you don't hear enough in sports. Pistons guard Richard Hamilton, who dazzled people in these NBA playoffs, got that good by realizing one day that he wasn't that good.

He was a teenager, attending one of those showcase camps for high school stars — the kind where college coaches lurk like vultures and shoe companies try to eagle-eye the next LeBron James. But unlike a lot of kids who watch their own moves, Hamilton spent his time looking around.

He saw players making rim-rattling jams. He saw players making long three-pointers. Those were both things he liked to do. And he silently congratulated himself, saying, "Man, I guess we're all gonna make the NBA."

Then one of the camp leaders gave a speech. A speech in which the real odds come out.

"He said maybe four kids out of the hundreds there might make the league one day," Hamilton, 26, recalls. "I couldn't believe it. When I heard that, I said, man, I gotta find something all these other guys aren't doing."

So Hamilton, who had been dribbling wildly past everyone his age, gravitated to a skill that the fewest players wanted. The mid-range jumper. The crowded, bumpy midrange jumper. The hard-to-gauge mid-range jumper. The sure-to-draw-an-elbow-or-an-eye-poke mid-range jumper. The eight-foot-to-20-foot mid-range jumper, just this side of the lane, just that side of the lane, halfway down this baseline, halfway down the other.

He staked it out like a homesteader.

And he made it his own.

He began with a drill on his hometown court, a concrete slab in Coatesville, Pa., a small town less than an hour from Philadelphia. "We had a McDonald's and a Dairy Queen, and that's it," Hamilton says. His court was purely small-town as well, metal rims and wooden backboards. Hamilton would throw the ball ahead, catch it, take one bounce, and shoot.

THE TEAM 39

Richard Hamilton wasn't blinded by success. He worked hard to achieve his athleticism. "Alcohol- and drug-free, you can run all day," Hamilton said. "My system's clean. Plus, I take pride in running and training myself."

KIRTHMON F. DOZIER

RICHARD HAMILTON

Position: Guard.
Age: 26.
Born: Feb. 14, 1978, Coatesville, Pa.
Height: 6-feet-7.
Weight: 193 pounds.
Drafted: First round (seventh overall) by Washington in 1999.
College: Connecticut.
NBA experience: 5 years.
How acquired: Traded from Washington with Hubert Davis and Bobby Simmons to Detroit for Jerry Stackhouse, Brian Cardinal and Ratko Varda in 2002.

STATISTICS

REGULAR SEASON

G	MIN	REB	AST	PTS
78	35.5	3.6	4.0	17.6

CAREER

G	MIN	REB	AST	PTS
372	30.9	3.2	2.7	16.9

NOTABLE

■ Wore a mask for most of the season after twice suffering a broken nose.

■ Helped win a championship in college, scoring 27 points to lead UConn past Duke in the 1999 NCAA title game and earning Final Four most outstanding player honors.

Photo on following page by KIRTHMON F. DOZIER

Richard Hamilton proves he can do more with a basketball than run around and make a jump shot.

Then he'd throw it someplace else, take one bounce and shoot.

In high school, he had a coach named Ricky Hicks, who would throw the ball all over the court. Run to it, one bounce, shoot. Run to it, one bounce, shoot.

Then, in college, at Connecticut, Hamilton advanced to two bounces. Run and get it, two bounces, shoot. Then a head fake thrown in. Bounce, head fake, shoot.

Every summer he came home to Coatesville, and he and Hicks would do it again. Countless hours. Countless days. Throw, fetch, shoot. Throw, dribble, shoot. Rip tried to stitch every inch of court into this routine, simulating any possible angle from which he could receive the ball. Get it. Pull up. Shoot.

Now, understand, this is not much fun. His contemporaries were practicing their windmill slams, or measuring their accuracy from the three-point line, throwing up their arms when they made one. That stuff is highlight reel. Jams. Treys. Who puts a 12-foot jumper on "SportsCenter"?

But there are a lot fewer guys who can sink those 12-foot jumpers than there are guys who can wham a ball down a rim. Hamilton's endless pull-up-and-shoot drills eventually made him familiar with every angle and every touch.

"The good thing when you pull up to shoot is that nobody knows where you're gonna do it but you," he says. "I figure half the time the guy can't stop on a dime and jump with me, so I'll get a clearer shot. And if they think you're going hard to the basket, they're gonna keep going even when you don't."

Rip: 'I'm in the best shape'

Rip Hamilton doesn't get tired. When he was in high school, his coach, Jim Smith, would make him run the sprint drills that every player hates. Hamilton laughed.

"He would tell me to run suicides," Hamilton said. "Bam, bam, bam, bam. I'm good. Bam, bam, bam, bam. I'm good. 'You can run me. I can do this all day.' "

Hamilton won't brag about his jump shot or his scoring average. But when talk turns to conditioning, he turns into Muhammad Ali.

"I honestly feel as though I'm in the best shape in the league," he said. "I know by the end of the game dudes are tired. That's when I get my second push."

How does he do it? Hamilton's grandfather on his dad's side, Edward Hamilton, was a distance runner. His uncle on his mom's side, Michael Long, ran in the Penn Relays.

Hamilton also adds an exercise regimen and a diet. And there are things he doesn't add.

"Alcohol- and drug-free, you can run all day," Hamilton said. "My system's clean. Plus, I take pride in running and training myself."

And Hamilton's father, Big Rip, taught him the value of nutrition.

"When I was like 10, 11 years old, he would always make sure I would drink a gallon of water and eat grapes and pineapples and apples before and after games," Hamilton said.

"I was like, 'The hell you got me drinking V8 juice?' " he said with a laugh. "I never understood it then, but I understand it now."

By Michael Rosenberg

THE SECOND SHIFT

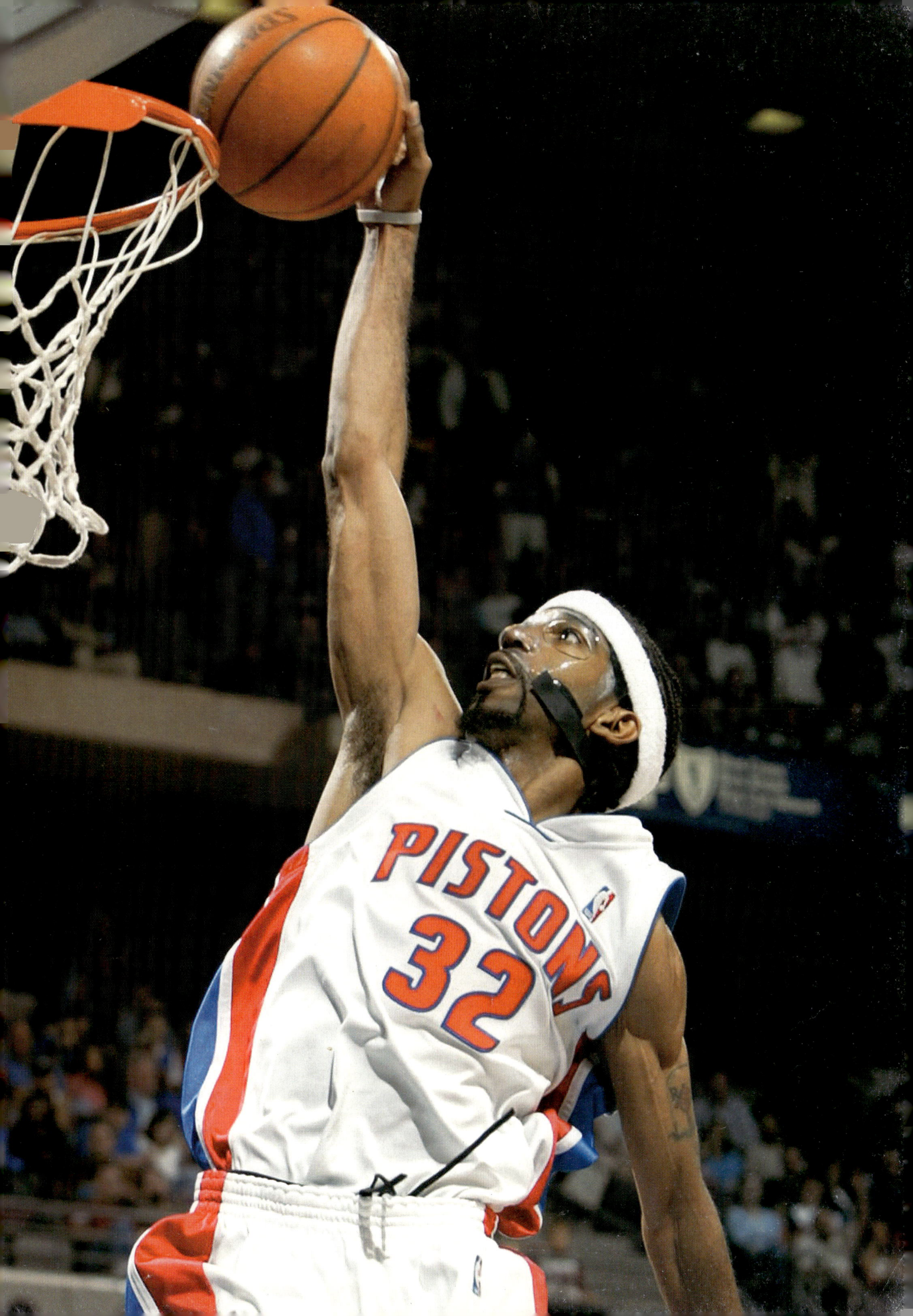
PISTONS
32

Fresh Prince
Quiet forward provides royal defense in second year

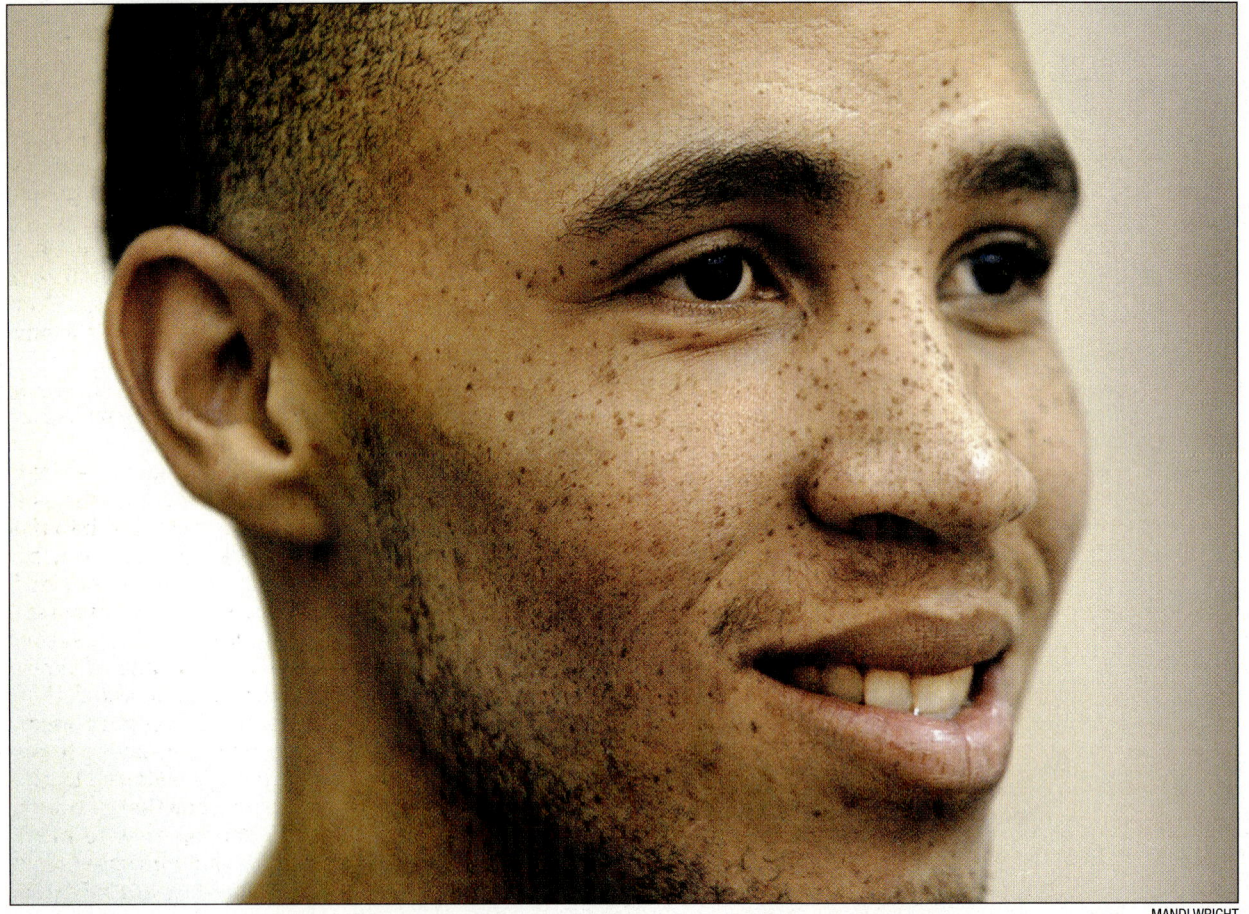

MANDI WRIGHT

The Pistons were counting on second-year forward Tayshaun Prince to continue to improve, and he rose to the occasion in the playoffs.

By Mitch Albom

Things we forget about Tayshaun Prince: 1) He is only 24. 2) He barely played last season as a rookie. 3) He is a college graduate. 4) While he looks like a cartoonishly skinny kid, he grew up in Compton, Calif., the hard side of L.A., which means 6) he really wanted to be drafted by the Lakers and 7) he went home and beat them.

Narrow your gaze on the player who could make a real difference in these championship finals. Everyone knows about Shaq, Kobe and Karl, and Rip, Ben and Rasheed. But Prince drew the defensive assignment on Kobe Bryant. Prince can get 20 in any game. And he can, like a magician

"When you have the president of your team saying he's confident in you, that knocks everything else off the table."
— **Pistons forward Tayshaun Prince**

with a rabbit, pull off something startling when you least expect it — a flying block, a baseline baby hook — that makes you stop and say, "How did he do that?"

"Have you shown your best stuff in this postseason yet?" I asked Prince after the Pistons advanced to play for the NBA crown.

"I definitely haven't," he said, as if grateful for the question. "I'm still waiting. And I'm pretty sure everybody else is waiting, too — especially with the attention I put on myself last year."

Believe it or not, he wonders what it would be like if he had stayed on the bench late last season, been brought along more slowly. Would the expectations this season be less? Would the disappointments never happen?

"I do sometimes think it would be better," he said, "but at the same time, I really had no choice. I didn't play the whole regular season. I had to go out there and try and make a statement, to say: 'Hey, I can play.' "

He was so impressive in the

THE SECOND SHIFT 42

playoffs last spring, people slammed Rick Carlisle for not playing him sooner. He was so impressive that when it came to using the No. 2 pick in the draft, president Joe Dumars passed on small forward Carmelo Anthony, essentially saying, "We already have a great young player at that position."

And then came sophomore year.

These have not been the playoffs of Tayshaun's dreams, let's be honest. After a terrific series against Milwaukee (he averaged 17.4 points and shot 59.3 percent), he had some goose-egg performances against the Nets and Pacers. He snapped at a reporter's question, saying, "How can you ask a player if he's losing his confidence?"

He sounded, and looked, like a player who was losing his confidence.

But looks — and sounds — can be deceiving. This is a kid who as a college junior threw his hat into the NBA draft, like so many others, then, suddenly, privately, decided he would wait. This is a guy who sat quietly his entire rookie season, knowing he was capable of doing more than he was being asked, then showed it when it counted most. This is a guy who, according to his critics, was being swallowed by the playoff pressure, but there he was, flying like a cannon shot to block Reggie Miller's shot and save Game 3 of the Indiana series. And there he was, stuffing Al Harrington in the tense closing moments to help save Game 6.

To the impatient observer who wants more shots, more points, more drives, Prince seemed to fade in these playoffs. But sometimes he was defending stars like Richard Jefferson. Sometimes he was being defended by the defensive player of the year, Ron Artest. And sometimes, yeah, he just wasn't at his best.

Still, he headed home to Los Angeles, where he was once named the best high school player in southern California. And remember, Prince not only starred in a big-time prep program, he also starred

ERIC SEALS
Prince — 6-foot-9 with an incredible wingspan — glides in for a dunk in the playoff opener against Milwaukee.

THE TEAM 43

Tayshaun Prince, known more throughout the playoffs for his stellar defense, drives for a basket against New Jersey's Richard Jefferson.

at big-time Kentucky, and he seems to calm down most when the insanity level rises.

"I know when to shut my phone off," he said of the Finals. "I know the task at hand."

When Dumars decided to forego Anthony in the draft, he called Prince and told him. Dumars is an understated guy. Prince is an understated guy. So not much needed to be said. But much was understood.

"I got his reading immediately," Prince recalled. "He was saying, 'I got faith in you.' That was huge. When you have the president of your team saying he's confident in you, that knocks everything else off the table. . . .

"I hear people now say, 'What if the Pistons had Carmelo? How well would they do?' But they don't understand, it would be a different situation than what Carmelo has in Denver. Denver needs him to play that offensive role. If he were here in Detroit, he wouldn't be getting all those plays called his way. He had a great year, so people are going to make those comparisons. But it's not the same situation."

In many ways, Prince saw this season as his rookie year. He played in only half the regular-season games in 2003 and started five of them. He averaged 3.3 points a game. He was a fill-in guy — until the playoffs, when he made a quick name for himself.

But he is still growing. Still learning. And occasionally, still stumbling. Looks can be deceiving. On the day Prince was drafted, he watched his stock fall from early first-rounder to late first-rounder. His skinny frame and the fact that he stayed in college four years were seen as negatives. (Don't get me started.) And so the Pistons nabbed him with the 23rd pick.

Prince's first thought was, if he was going to fall that far, he wanted to fall all the way to pick No. 27, the Lakers.

The second thought he expressed later: "I'm going to make a statement. Everybody's going to know, sooner or later, that they made the wrong move."

And this Prince made a statement to earn his own crown.

TAYSHAUN PRINCE

Position: Forward.
Age: 24.
Born: Feb. 28, 1980, Compton, Calif.
Height: 6-feet-9.
Weight: 215 pounds.
Drafted: First round (23rd overall) by Detroit in 2002.
College: Kentucky.
NBA experience: 2 years.

STATISTICS

REGULAR SEASON

G	MIN	REB	AST	PTS
82	32.9	4.8	2.3	10.3

CAREER

G	MIN	REB	AST	PTS
124	25.3	3.5	1.7	7.9

NOTABLE

■ The Prince of the Palace will long be remembered for using his incredible wingspan to block a Reggie Miller would-be lay-up late in Game 2 of the Eastern Conference finals, saving a Pistons victory.

■ Scored a career-high 25 points in a 101-89 victory at Orlando on April 10.

■ Grabbed a career-high 11 rebounds — all defensive — in an 87-83 win over Miami on Dec. 3.

■ His 21-footer from the right corner in the waning seconds of Game 6 was considered to be the knockout blow to the Pacers.

THE SECOND SHIFT

Don't forget the Memo

Okur, Brown finally on the same page

By Jo-Ann Barnas

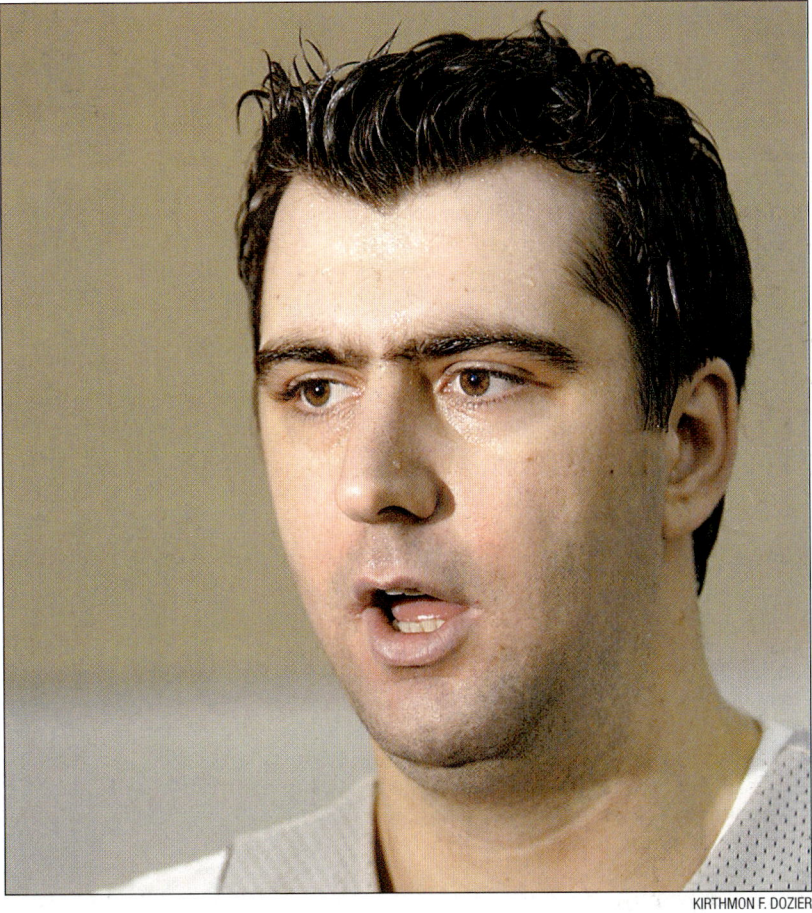

It was a routine basket, a hook shot on an assist from Richard Hamilton. But that didn't matter. Mehmet Okur looked over and saw the response — teammates leaping from their seats, celebrating his first two points in the second quarter of the Pistons' Game 4 victory against the Milwaukee Bucks in the first round of the NBA playoffs.

"They just erupted for him," coach Larry Brown said with a smile. "They recognize I've been on Memo, trying to coach him, and they were letting him know that they're supportive of him."

From starter to sub, from feeling up to down to back up again, Okur has described himself as "totally accepting" of his reserve role since the Pistons acquired Rasheed Wallace.

That's because he knows what has happened with this team.

"We're better," he said. "And I've become so focused." That's good news for Brown, who needs Okur.

"I tell him all the time, 'The respect I have for you is shared by everybody in the league,'" Brown said. "And I keep telling him that because people recognize he's on a winning team, and the contribution he's making to help us win will be something that's so significant when this year ends. Not only from our standpoint, but the standpoint of his value. But it's hard for him sometimes because people are telling him, 'You have to get numbers.'"

Okur, who can become a restricted free agent after this season, said he knows he has the support of Brown and management. Okur, a native of Florya, Turkey, was the first foreign-born player drafted by the Pistons. He was selected in the second round of the 2001 draft, but he spent the following season with his Turkish team.

After joining the Pistons in 2002-03, he gained confidence — especially in the playoffs — under former coach Rick Carlisle. During the 2003-04 regular season, Okur averaged 9.6 points in 71 games, with 33 starts.

He saw less action in the playoffs. But his scoring off the bench helped the Pistons in several games.

Brown and Okur agree that the communication problems they experienced diminished as the season progressed. At nearly 7 feet, Okur is among the most athletic players on the team.

On the court, Okur has a deadly shot from the perimeter, but Brown wanted to make him a stronger inside player, posting up for shots.

"I'll give you an example," Brown said. "I'm always yelling at him to run, and he thinks he is running. But what I'm saying is, really sprint."

Okur said of Brown: "He's trying to push me, yelling at me all the time, because he wants me to do it the right way. He's trying to make

Mehmet Okur's minutes were sporadic in the playoffs. The Turkish native will become a free agent after this season.

"He's trying to push me, yelling at me all the time, because he wants me to do it the right way. He's trying to make me a good player in this league.
— Pistons forward/center Mehmet Okur

Ben Wallace and Mehmet Okur do a little dance before Game 7 of the Eastern Conference semifinals against the Nets. The dance worked — the Pistons blew out the Nets, 90-69.

MEHMET OKUR

Position: Forward/center.
Age: 25.
Born: May 26, 1979, Florya, Turkey.
Height: 6-feet-11.
Weight: 249 pounds.
Drafted: 2nd round (38th overall) by Detroit in 2001.
College: None.
NBA experience: 2 years.

STATISTICS
REGULAR SEASON

G	MIN	REB	AST	PTS
71	22.3	5.9	1.0	9.6

CAREER

G	MIN	REB	AST	PTS
143	20.6	5.3	1.0	8.2

NOTABLE

■ With his playing time diminished since the acquisition of Rasheed Wallace, Okur's point totals decreased in the playoffs after a regular season in which he averaged nearly 10 points.

■ A catalyst in the Pistons' tide-turning Game 2 victory against the Pacers, Okur had nine points and four rebounds in the first half, helping the Pistons rally from a nine-point deficit.

■ Scored a career-high 27 points in a 95-91 win over Toronto on Jan. 14.

■ A restricted free agent after the season, a host of teams — foremost among them New York and Dallas — are said to be highly interested in signing him.

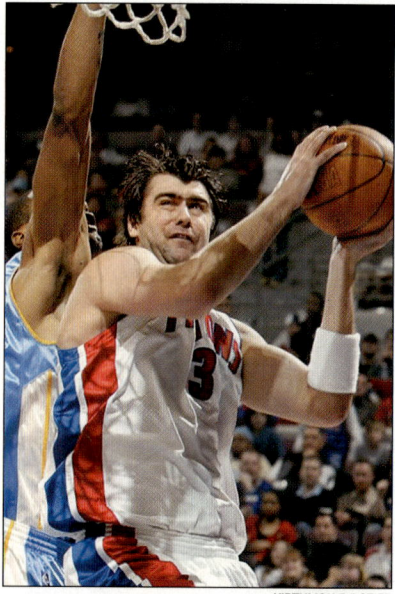

Mehmet Okur will be a free agent after this season. The Pistons hope to re-sign Okur, who can emerge as a reliable 18-point, 10-rebound player.

me a good player in this league. I know what he wants from me now. He wants me to play first underneath, then outside."

In two years in Michigan, Okur made a lot of adjustments. His English improved tremendously.

He discovered several Middle Eastern restaurants that he enjoys.

He said he liked sushi the first time he tried it.

In the summer of 2004, he planned to marry his girlfriend, Yeliz Caliskan, in Turkey. She was expected to return with him next season.

"See, I'm getting used to life here," Okur said. "And I don't get lost anymore on the roads."

He and Brown are on the same page, too.

After one practice during the playoffs, Brown worked one-on-one for 10 minutes with Okur on his inside moves.

"Drop, step, go! Go hard!" Brown said.

A few minutes later: "Run and do a jump hook."

And then, a few minutes after that: "You know the one that I get mad at you, on defense?"

Okur demonstrated the move — the right way.

"Good, Memo," Brown said, ending the session with a laugh.

THE SECOND SHIFT 46

Mr. team player

Williamson knows the deal and gets it done

Corliss Williamson provided valuable playing time in the playoffs, especially when Ben and Rasheed Wallace got in early foul trouble.

By Mitch Albom

It's not that Corliss Williamson is patient. He hates sitting in traffic.

He'll rap on the dashboard and mutter under his breath. When his wife is taking too long to get ready, he'll stand behind her in the bathroom, tapping his foot as loudly as he can.

"Does that work?" he is asked.

"Not really," he says.

See? There you go. He's not patient — but he knows the deal.

And being a great bench player is all about knowing the deal.

Williamson, a 6-foot-7 forward, came to the Pistons in February 2001 as part of the trade that sent Jerome Williams and Eric Montross to Toronto. In 2002, he won the NBA's Sixth Man award.

It's a noble job, being a bench player. Whereas glory hounds assume a bench man must be lacking something, they are only partially right.

The truth is, a great bench player has to lack something: He has to lack ego. He has to lack resentment. He has to lack the demons of "Why aren't I out there?" and "How come so-and-so is starting and not me?"

He has to lack a sense of entitlement. But then, Williamson has never had much use for that. As the grandson of an Arkansas janitor who worked 12-hour shifts in order to start his own cleaning business, Corliss was taught a simple philosophy: You work for what you get, and you get what you work for.

"I feel like I've found a home here in Detroit."
— **Pistons forward Corliss Williamson**

When he arrived in Detroit in 2001, it was his second trade in one season. His contract was ending. Free agency loomed. Teams were unloading him — to avoid being left holding the bag.

"You've got two months here to show us what you've got," Joe Dumars, the Pistons' president, told Williamson back then. "Or at the very least, to show some other team what you've got."

He knew the deal, got the deal done on the court, and won another deal — a six-year contract worth $32.5 million.

Corliss Williamson needed his "Big Nasty" demeanor during the physical series against the Pacers.

CORLISS WILLIAMSON

Position: Forward.
Age: 30.
Born: Dec. 4, 1973, Russellville, Ark.
Height: 6-feet-7.
Weight: 245 pounds.
Drafted: 1st round (13th overall) by Sacramento in 1995.
College: Arkansas.
NBA experience: 9 years.
How acquired: With Kornel David, Tyrone Corbin and first-round pick from Toronto for Jerome Williams and Eric Montross in 2001.

STATISTICS

REGULAR SEASON

G	MIN	REB	AST	PTS
79	19.9	3.2	0.7	9.5

CAREER

G	MIN	REB	AST	PTS
645	24.1	4.1	1.3	11.9

NOTABLE

■ Nicknamed Big Nasty for his size and rugged play.

■ Also won a championship in college, leading Arkansas to a 76-72 victory over Grant Hill-led Duke in the 1994 NCAA title game and earning Final Four most outstanding player honors.

■ Named NBA Sixth Man of the Year in 2002.

■ Ranked in the top 10 in field-goal percentage (.505), but did not make a three-pointer all season.

He knew the deal in college, too. As a sophomore, he helped the Arkansas Razorbacks win the 1994 NCAA title, and he was named the Most Outstanding Player of the tournament. Then he decided, over a chorus of boosters, to stay in school for his junior season.

"I don't have the mental attitude right now for the life of an NBA player," he said at the time, a remarkably candid assessment for a 20-year-old.

He knew the deal in Sacramento, when, after four years there, he was a free agent faced with leaving or taking a cut-rate, one-year contract, because the Kings were out of money. He chose the latter, delighting fans and confounding experts.

And he knows the deal now, as he counts the minutes in the first quarter, waiting for the horn, his entrance, and the Pistons' shift to his banging, post-up presence.

"I feel like I've found a home here in Detroit," Williamson said after winning the Sixth Man award.

Williamson looks a lot like Adrian Dantley minus the attitude. Dantley was a back-it-up post player, much like Williamson. And if he didn't score, he'd get to the line, same as Corliss.

But Williamson is less selfish. And when it comes to leg strength, this guy is a tree trunk. Backing him up is tough. Stopping him from backing up is tougher.

He has been nicknamed "Big Nasty" ever since he executed a dunk in junior high.

Now, he gets a lot of the "nasty" baskets inside when Detroit needs offense.

But his minutes decreased in the 2003-04 season. The acquisition of Rasheed Wallace and the growth of Mehmet Okur made the Pistons less dependent on Williamson.

In his ninth season, Williamson struggled to reach double figures in points. Only in his rookie year — when he averaged 11.5 minutes in Sacramento — did Williamson fall short of 10 points per game for a full season. This season, he averaged 9.5.

But it doesn't matter. Life is not about trophies or points or minutes. It's about knowing the deal and ignoring the rest. Here's to Williamson and all that he lacks, No. 34 on your roster, a team player in your hearts.

THE SECOND SHIFT

Living for his brother

Tragic death fuels Pistons' Hunter

By Jo-Ann Barnas

I grabbed him around his neck and I said, 'You know, I'm the bigger brother and I'll always be the bigger brother. But sometimes you make me want to strangle you.' "

"He said, 'You make me want to strangle you, too!' "

"And I kissed him on his forehead. I said, 'But I love you.' He said, 'I love you, too.'

"That was the last thing we exchanged. Of course, God knew what was going on. But I didn't, and we didn't."

Until last summer, Pistons guard Lindsey Hunter said he wouldn't have been able to share that story, the last conversation he had with his brother, Tommie, on the day he died.

Living with his passing isn't any easier now than it was in June 2001, when 19-year-old Tommie borrowed Lindsey's SUV to visit friends one evening and never came home. He was killed in a one-car accident near Jackson, Miss., four months before he was to begin his freshman year playing basketball at Jackson State, Lindsey's alma mater, following in his older brother's footsteps.

But to Lindsey, it was always the other way around.

"I was already thinking then what I was going to do when I retire: Follow Tommie around going to his games," he said. "He was like a son to me because I was 11 years older. I basically raised him from diapers up. I dressed him. I took him to kindergarten and first grade. All the way up."

Maybe you've noticed the number on Hunter's back. For the first eight years of his NBA career, starting in 1993 when the Pistons made him a first-round draft pick, he wore No. 1.

He wears 10 now. Tommie's number.

Hunter first wore it in 2001-02, his only season with the Los Angeles Lakers — two seasons after the Pistons traded him the

Lindsey Hunter displayed his lock-down defense in the playoffs, including this steal against New Jersey's Lucious Harris.

> "God has blessed me to play this long. ... If we can win a title here, it would be so much fun."
> — Pistons guard Lindsey Hunter

Lindsey Hunter pestered New Jersey's Jason Kidd into one of his poorest playoff performances in the Eastern semifinals.

first time.

Known for his aggressive defense, Hunter will never forget his overwhelming sense of joy in being part of the Lakers' NBA championship. He also will never forget the road it took to get there. For Hunter, a memorable moment came in Game 7 of the Western Conference finals against Sacramento, when coach Phil Jackson summoned him off the bench to guard Mike Bibby with these words: "Get in. Get him."

Hunter felt the strength of two people in that game. Now, almost two years later, he has that feeling again.

Anyone who saw him play in the first round of the playoffs against Milwaukee would believe that.

Before a sellout crowd at the Palace, the Pistons beat the Bucks, 108-82, in their playoff opener. A big reason was a razor-sharp defense that forced 25 turnovers.

Hunter, who entered the game in the second quarter with playoff newcomer Mike James, scored on a three-pointer and finished with three of the Pistons' team-playoff-record 14 steals. The two were relentless, pestering the Bucks' shooters like hungry vultures.

"Tommie, he's here with me every day, every game," Hunter said. "To lose him the way it happened, I remember I was ready to retire. I didn't because I knew the type of person he was. I had to stick it out. I had to fight through those hard times."

Now in his 11th season, Hunter knows he has come full circle.

After playing his first eight seasons in Detroit, he was traded to Milwaukee for Billy Owens in June 2000. He took on a supporting role and helped the Bucks make it to the Eastern Conference finals.

The Bucks traded him to the Lakers the next season, when he started more than half of the regular-season games, averaging 5.8 points.

Then Hunter was traded to Toronto, where he played sparingly last season because of injuries.

The Pistons reacquired him last fall, trading Michael Curry to Toronto. Hunter played 11 games, missing 44 with a strained right hamstring.

Then he left the Pistons again Feb. 19, when they traded him and Chucky Atkins to Boston as part of a three-team deal that brought Rasheed Wallace to Detroit. Six days later, Hunter returned as a free agent.

"God has blessed me to play this long," he said. "I'm a 6-2 guard, and I've been able to keep focused on bigger and better things. I've won a championship, and I have an opportunity to win another one. If we can win a title here, it would be so much fun."

LINDSEY HUNTER

Position: Guard.
Age: 33.
Born: Dec. 3, 1970, Utica, Miss.
Height: 6-feet-2.
Weight: 195 pounds.
Drafted: 1st round (10th overall) by Detroit in 1993.
College: Jackson State.
NBA experience: 11 years.
How acquired: Started season with Pistons, traded to Boston in three-team deal that brought Rasheed Wallace and Mike James to Detroit, then claimed off waivers from the Celtics on Feb. 19.

STATISTICS
REGULAR SEASON

G	MIN	REB	AST	PTS
33	20.0	2.0	2.6	3.5

CAREER

G	MIN	REB	AST	PTS
714	28.6	2.5	3.0	10.1

NOTABLE

■ A tenacious on-the-ball defender and sparkplug reserve, Hunter also won a ring with the Lakers in 2002, when L.A. swept New Jersey.

■ Plans someday to teach elementary education in his home state of Mississippi.

GREAT EXPECTATIONS

When Jackson State guard Lindsey Hunter was chosen by the Pistons as the 10th pick in the 1993 draft, he was expected to be the next Isiah Thomas.

"This is just a dream come true. I've always admired Isiah Thomas, and I want to play just like Isiah Thomas. He's an incredible guy, and I want to be just like him," Hunter said on draft night.

The Pistons took Tennessee guard Allan Houston with the next pick — forming a Isiah-Joe Dumars-esque backcourt duo.

Columnist Charlie Vincent wrote in the Free Press that year: "Hunter is the Thomas clone, quick and certain of himself, with the hands of a magician, making a basketball disappear before a defender's eyes. He has Thomas' smile and, suppressed just below the surface, a touch of Thomas' combativeness, too."

But Hunter never lived up to the giant expectations, and Houston bolted to the Knicks as a free agent in 1996.

Hold on. It turns out the man who was supposed to replace the two-time NBA champ Thomas is a two-time champion, too. After winning a title with the Lakers in 2002, Hunter now has two rings. And he won with the Pistons.

Just like Isiah.

By Mark Francescutti

Learning curve

It's Darko mania as rookie soaks up American culture

By Mark Francescutti

Darko Milicic took time adjusting to American life through concerts, restaurants and getting his television to work.

His English is improving, though it's still a little broken in a heavy accent.

He bought a house in Oakland Township, about 10 minutes from the Palace, but he said he hasn't made any extravagant purchases since signing an $11-million contract with the Pistons.

"Yeah, great house," Milicic said. "It's a new area. Not a lot of houses. Just three, four, five houses."

Milicic, the No. 2 overall pick in the NBA draft, came to the Pistons this past summer from Serbia-Montenegro.

Coach Larry Brown jokes that Milicic's biggest concern is getting his driver's license. Milicic, who turned 18 last June, received his license late in 2003. In the first part of the season, he had to hitch rides with Chauncey Billups to and from practice and the airport. The two had long talks.

"He asks me about Serbia a lot of times," Milicic said. " 'What would you be doing over there?' And I ask him things about the league. I appreciate it."

Milicic likes his cable television, but "I've had problems with it," he said. "I am trying to watch TV, and I cannot see the channel, and I got to call somebody."

Ask him about food, and Milicic perks up.

"Chicken and beef, chicken and beef," he said of his favorite foods.

His favorite restaurant is Bravo! Cucina Italiana in Rochester Hills, located a few miles from his home. Not surprisingly, restaurant manager Mike Zahorchak said Milicic orders the chicken griglia, a wood-grilled chicken topped with lemon butter sauce.

One time, "he was in here with a nice-looking young lady for lunch," Zahorchak said in October. "That was a new one. The staff loves him. He's just a nice guy."

Milicic has been to concerts — Red Hot Chili Peppers and Bryan Adams — though he left the Peppers concert early.

"I go out after two songs," Milicic said. "I like, but it was my first time at concert. ... I cannot see a lot of the times."

Milicic is 7-feet.

Though his progress on the court was slow, Milicic became a fan favorite throughout the season.

Darko Milicic's playing time was relegated to blowout victories and losses in his rookie season. He was nicknamed the "Human Victory Cigar."

"It feels the best. When fans like you, it's great."
— **Pistons center Darko Milicic**

THE TEAM 51

He was nicknamed, "The Human Victory Cigar," because he usually entered games in blowout victories. Despite not becoming an immediate star like fellow top picks LeBron James and Carmelo Anthony, the Palace fans' support of Milicic never wavered.

"It feels the best," Milicic said. "When fans like you, it's great."

Brown has made it clear he knew that Milicic wasn't going to play much this season. Informed of Brown's outlook, Milicic said he would continue to work hard but that his patience wouldn't last forever.

"Next year," he said, "I have to play."

Rookie Darko Milicic poses with his car in the Palace parking lot.

JULIAN H. GONZALEZ

Driving with Darko

QUESTION: What cars do you own, and why did you select those?

ANSWER: An Audi A8 and a BMW X5. It's my first time buying, and they were not too expensive (the A8 starts at $69,220, the X5 at $41,495), not too bad for first time. After this, I'm going to go a little bit better.

Q: What was the hardest question on the written exam?

A: I had to answer one about if I have a trailer and have to stop in the middle of the road, what am I supposed to do first — something about looking behind me, around me, signal . . .

Q: How did you do on your test?

A: Good. I passed the first time.

Q: How did you learn to drive?

A: I never took lessons. I just tried it for three days in my friend's car and then it was easy.

Q: You are 7 feet tall. Was it hard to find a car you could fit in?

A: It's hard, yes. Mercedes-Benz, I think is best for big guys. So that is what I am going to get next. An S600. It's V12, 493 horsepower. It's very impressive. I've never seen a car with space like this.

Q: Have you gotten any speeding tickets yet?

A: Yep. Two. I can't drive slow.

By Helene St. James

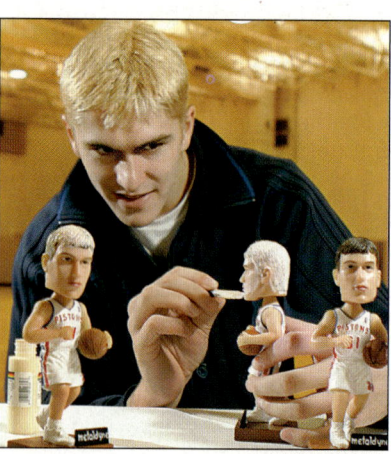

DARKO MILICIC

Position: Forward/center.
Age: 18.
Born: June 20, 1985, Novi Sad, Serbia-Montenegro.
Height: 7-feet.
Weight: 250 pounds.
Drafted: 1st round (second overall) by Detroit in 2003.
College: None.
NBA experience: Rookie.

STATISTICS

REGULAR SEASON
G	MIN	REB	AST	PTS
34	4.7	1.3	0.2	1.4

CAREER
G	MIN	REB	AST	PTS
34	4.7	1.3	0.2	1.4

NOTABLE

■ Dyed his hair blond before a Darko bobblehead promotion at the Palace, then hand-painted the hair on several of the dolls, given randomly to fans entering the arena.

■ Nicknamed the "Human Victory Cigar" because he usually entered the game in Pistons blowout victories.

■ Sandwiched between high school phenom LeBron James and Syracuse sensation Carmelo Anthony in the 2003 draft.

■ One of four players drafted by the Pistons — along with Lindsey Hunter, Mehmet Okur and Tayshaun Prince — currently on the team's roster.

JULIAN H. GONZALEZ

Darko Milicic uses paint to lighten the hair on his bobbleheads after he dyed his hair blond.

The Elden statesman

Campbell dodging bad guys, roadkill

Elden Campbell gave the Pistons a shot-blocking presence off the bench, like he did here to the Pacers' Al Harrington.

JULIAN H. GONZALEZ

ELDEN CAMPBELL

Position: Center/forward.
Age: 35.
Born: July 23, 1968, Los Angeles.
Height: 7-feet.
Weight: 279 pounds.
Drafted: 1st round (27th overall) by L.A. Lakers in 1990.
College: Clemson.
NBA experience: 14 years.
How acquired: Signed with Detroit as a free agent in 2003.

STATISTICS

REGULAR SEASON

G	MIN	REB	AST	PTS
65	13.7	3.2	0.7	5.6

CAREER

G	MIN	REB	AST	PTS
1,004	25.3	6.0	1.2	10.6

NOTABLE

■ A key frontcourt reserve for the Pistons, the well-traveled Campbell played eight-plus seasons with the Lakers, then made stops in Charlotte, New Orleans and Seattle before arriving in Detroit.

■ In 1997, became the seventh player in NBA history to increase his scoring average in each of his first seven seasons.

■ Appeared in the NBA Finals with the Lakers as a rookie in 1991, losing to Chicago.

■ Nicknamed "Easy." Campbell played in his 1,000th NBA game earlier this season in a 79-61 win over Indiana.

By Mark Francescutti

Meet Elden Campbell. At 35, he's the oldest Piston, but he might be a teenager trapped in a man's body.

Rookie Darko Milicic, 18, doesn't play video games. Campbell? He's a video game veteran. The Pistons' new center says he owns almost every video game system, but his favorite is Nintendo's GameCube.

He's button-jamming right now on a game called "Dead to Rights," in which he plays Jack Slate, a cop, along with trusty attack dog Shadow, as they shoot and obliterate just about everything on the screen. He says his next challenge is "Hunter: the Reckoning," in which Campbell chooses to play a biker ex-con, rave party girl, female ex-cop or prison priest to battle monsters that want to destroy the world.

"Then I play Mario Party 4" — an E-rated game — "with my little kids," Campbell said.

Campbell is also computer savvy. He said he studied computers at Clemson and loves his humongous, 17-inch Apple laptop. He surfs the Internet regularly. His homepage is CNN.com, because, "I don't want to read about (sports). I come here and live it every day.

"I'm an indoors guy and an electronics guy," Campbell said. "I like to fish, (but) this time of year, I'm forced inside. Hate the cold, but I'll sacrifice to be a Piston. I've been blessed to play in warmer climates."

Campbell played almost nine seasons with the Los Angeles Lakers before being traded to Charlotte. Then, in a little more than a year, he has moved three times. "Too many," he said.

First the Hornets moved to New Orleans. Then Campbell was traded to Seattle in February. He signed a two-year, $8.4-million contract with the Pistons in July.

Campbell and his wife, Rosemary, have a home near the Palace and children ages 1-6: son Jayle and daughters Jael and Arial.

He said he was "pleasantly surprised with the area."

"Coming home and see some deer running around out the window — that's the thing I like. I guess the downside is that you see all kinds of animals on the side of the road. There's roadkill everywhere. Luckily, I haven't hit anything yet."

Campbell describes himself as a "family man" and a "Christian man." His nickname is "Easy," for his easygoing, professional personality.

After starting early in the season, Campbell's minutes dwindled. But he played a role as a big presence in the middle throughout the playoffs. He even hit a couple turnarounds in the post every now and then.

THE TEAM 53

Glad to be here

With Pistons, James plays less and enjoys it more

Mike James, driving on Milwaukee's Erick Strickland in the first round, often spelled Chauncey Billups after his acquisition from the Celtics late in the regular season.

KIRTHMON F. DOZIER

MIKE JAMES

Position: Guard.
Age: 28.
Born: June 23, 1975, Amityville, N.Y.
Height: 6-feet-2.
Weight: 188 pounds.
Drafted: Not drafted.
College: Duquesne.
NBA experience: 3 years.
How acquired: Traded from Boston to Detroit in a three-team deal that also sent Rasheed Wallace from Atlanta to Detroit in 2004.

STATISTICS

REGULAR SEASON

G	MIN	REB	AST	PTS
81	27.1	2.9	4.2	9.3

CAREER

G	MIN	REB	AST	PTS
174	23.2	2.3	3.5	8.1

NOTABLE

■ Little was known about him when he came from Boston in the three-team deal that also brought Rasheed Wallace to Detroit, but James fit right in and became a valuable backcourt reserve, providing energy and reliable defense off the bench.

■ Started 55 games for the Celtics in 2003-04, averaging 10.7 points and 4.4 assists, before getting traded to Detroit.

■ After playing college ball at Duquesne, James played professionally in Austria and France before signing with Miami in 2001.

By Terrance Collins

Mike James should have been happier in Boston. He was a starter there; he rode the bench in Detroit. He played a ton of minutes there; he played a lot less in Detroit. He was the first option to run the offense there; he was the fourth in Detroit.

He should have been happier in Boston. But he didn't win in Boston. He won a title in Detroit.

"It felt good," James said after making the first playoff appearance of his three-year career. "The atmosphere was exciting. It was great to get out there. There were a little jitters. I was excited."

James, who was part of a seven-player, three-team trade in February 2004, was excited about the opportunity to play for Detroit, too.

James' excitement turned into tenacity, which led the Pistons to call him and teammate Lindsey Hunter the team's "pit bulls."

"We know our minutes are limited, so we're going to pick up our aggressiveness on defense and try to make our defense create offense for us and get easy baskets," James said.

After a season and a half of trying to establish himself in the league, James found his stride in Boston this season. But the Celtics struggled to a 23-32 record.

Then James became a by-product in a trade that brought Rasheed Wallace to the Pistons.

Good, old-fashioned hard work got it done for James. He wasn't drafted out of tiny Duquesne, but he stayed with it. He played in Austria and France before joining the Miami Heat in 2001.

James averaged 6.3 points and 3.7 assists with the Pistons during the regular season. He helped shut down New Jersey's Jason Kidd in the conference semifinals.

Sure, James should have been happier in Boston. But he can't be happier than being a champion.

THE SECOND SHIFT 54

Full circle

Journeyman Ham fits in with homestate team

Saginaw High's Darvin Ham provided spark off the bench during the regular season and playoffs. Ham has also played for Denver, Indiana, Washington, Milwaukee and Atlanta.

KIRTHMON F. DOZIER

By Terrance Collins

Small forward Darvin Ham felt right at home with the Pistons.

That's not just because the seven-year veteran from Saginaw returned to play for the team he grew up watching.

In playing for Denver, Indiana, Milwaukee and Atlanta, Ham made a name for himself in the league with his high energy off the bench, tenacious defense and strong athleticism, not for his offense.

So it's no wonder Ham, as a reserve, fit so comfortably into coach Larry Brown's defense-oriented system.

"I'm just excited to be a part of this team," said Ham, who as a kid came to the Silverdome with his uncle to watch the Pistons play.

"I know people have been talking about our offense and not being on the same page as Coach (Brown), but when I was in Milwaukee, offense was the last thing we worried about under George Karl. We concentrated on stopping our opponent, rebounding and winning the free-throw battle."

The Pistons ranked 24th in the 29-team league in scoring (90.1) in the regular season, but finished tied for first with San Antonio in fewest points allowed (84.3). They also led the league in blocks per game with 6.95.

When the Pistons struggled with Brown's system early in the season, Ham knew what needed to be done for the team to be successful.

"We just have to get back to playing Piston basketball: tough defense, rebound the basketball and play unselfish," Ham said.

Ham played in 54 games during the season, averaging 1.8 points and 1.7 rebounds. He started two games.

"He dominates practice," Brown said. "I just think that kind of effort should be rewarded."

Now Ham can rest easy, knowing he helped the Pistons win the ultimate award — an NBA championship.

DARVIN HAM

Position: Forward.
Age: 30.
Born: July 23, 1973, Saginaw.
Height: 6-feet-7.
Weight: 240 pounds.
Drafted: Never drafted.
College: Texas Tech.
NBA experience: 7 years.
How acquired: Signed as a free agent in 2003.

STATISTICS
REGULAR SEASON

G	MIN	REB	AST	PTS
54	9.0	1.7	0.3	1.8

CAREER

G	MIN	REB	AST	PTS
370	13.3	2.5	0.6	3.0

NOTABLE
■ Featured on the cover of Sports Illustrated shattering a backboard during Texas Tech's upset of North Carolina in the 1996 NCAA tournament.

■ Darvin's mother, Wilmer Jones-Ham, is the mayor of Saginaw.

TREMAINE FOWLKES

Position: Forward.
Age: 28.
Born: April 11, 1976, Los Angeles.
Height: 6-feet-6.
Weight: 198 pounds.
Drafted: Second round (54th overall) by Denver in 1998.
College: Fresno State.
NBA experience: 3 years.
How acquired: Signed as a free agent in 2003.

STATISTICS
REGULAR SEASON

G	MIN	REB	AST	PTS
36	7.3	1.5	0.4	1.2

CAREER

G	MIN	REB	AST	PTS
95	12.4	2.3	0.6	3.0

NOTABLE
■ Reserve left off playoff roster.

■ Became the first alum of the National Basketball Development League to start an NBA game, February 2002 against Memphis.

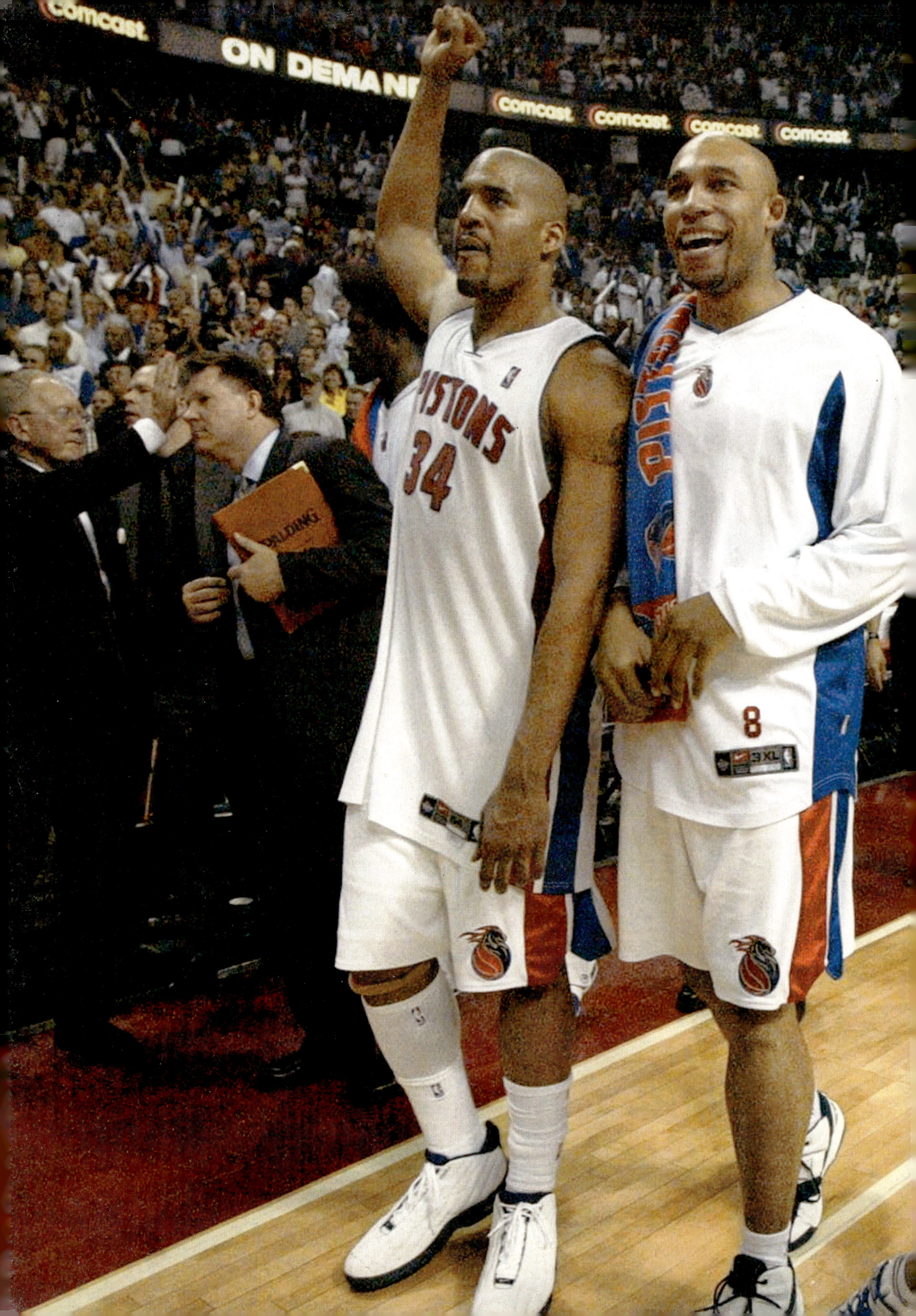
comcast
comcast
comcast
comcast
comcast
PISTONS
34
8

THE THIRD SHIFT

THE PLAYOFFS

| 108 | PISTONS | ROUND 1 | GAME 1 | SERIES 1-0 | BUCKS | 82 |
| 92 | BUCKS | ROUND 1 | GAME 2 | SERIES 1-1 | PISTONS | 89 |

Split decision

Pistons shine and falter in two games at Palace

By Perry A. Farrell

GAME 1

AUBURN HILLS *(APRIL 18, 2004)* — In a devastating defensive performance, the Pistons set a team playoff record with 14 steals and scored 28 points off 25 turnovers.

That helped the Pistons take a 1-0 series lead.

The Pistons led, 52-43, at halftime after forcing nine turnovers and blocking four shots. They led by as many as 30 points in the second half.

Richard Hamilton led the Pistons with 21 points. Tayshaun Prince had 14 points, 11 rebounds and four blocked shots.

Chauncey Billups returned after missing the final four games of the regular season with a left ankle injury. He scored 12.

Milwaukee was without its best point guard, rookie T.J. Ford, who is out with a bruised spinal cord. Ford's backups, Damon Jones and Brevin Knight, combined for 11 points and five turnovers.

Michael Redd, the team's leading scorer during the regular season with a 21.7-point average, scored 11 points and committed seven turnovers.

GAME 2

AUBURN HILLS *(APRIL 21, 2004)* — The game literally slipped out of the Pistons' hands when the ball sailed out of Rasheed Wallace's hands and out of bounds as he set up for a potential winning three-pointer with 4.1 seconds left.

Milwaukee evened the series at 1, getting better performances from Redd, who scored 26 points, and bench player Toni Kukoc, who shot 7-for-8 from the field.

"It definitely was a wake-up call," said Billups, who scored 20 points.

Detroit's 11-game home winning streak ended after Hamilton was ejected with 4:58 upon receiving his second technical foul. Hamilton, who scored 18 points, threw his facemask across the floor.

The Pistons made only six of 25 three-pointers and got pounded on the boards, 48-37. They also got a scoreless performance from the bench until 2:58 remained in the fourth quarter.

KIRTHMON F. DOZIER
Ben Wallace dunks past Milwaukee's Joe Smith in the second quarter of Game 1 of the first-round series. The Pistons set a team playoff record with 14 steals in the 108-82 victory.

Photo on previous pages by KIRTHMON F. DOZIER
After winning in the playoffs, you can celebrate with a yell or a wave. Rasheed Wallace, right, lets it all out. Corliss Williamson, left, and Darvin Ham take it more in stride.

THE THIRD SHIFT 58

| 95 PISTONS | ROUND 1 GAME 3 | SERIES 2-1 | BUCKS | 85 |
| 109 PISTONS | ROUND 1 GAME 4 | SERIES 3-1 | BUCKS | 92 |

Old Milwaukee

Pistons take two in beer town, 3-1 series lead

By Free Press staff and news services

GAME 3

MILWAUKEE (APRIL 24, 2004) — The Pistons shut down Milwaukee during the final four minutes for a 2-1 series lead.

After allowing 30 points in the first period, Detroit needed a 23-4 run at the start of the second half to take its first lead of the game.

Then the defense took over, holding Milwaukee to only a free throw in the final four minutes.

Coach Larry Brown called the second half the Pistons' best defensive effort of the series.

Ben Wallace, limited by foul trouble in the first half, scored 11 of his 13 points in the second. He also had 21 rebounds. Chauncey Billups scored 21 points.

"We had a good opportunity and let it slip away," Bucks forward Joe Smith said.

GAME 4

MILWAUKEE (APRIL 26, 2004) — Unselfish throughout the contest, the Pistons racked up 31 assists, shot 57 percent from the field and got 27 points from Richard Hamilton in the victory.

Rasheed Wallace chipped in 20 points and nine rebounds, and Tayshaun Prince scored 17 on 8-for-11 shooting.

"I don't think we can play better," Brown said. "I feel a lot better today than I did when we were coming over here."

The Pistons were 20-for-21 from the free-throw line.

Michael Redd shot 5-for-19 and scored 12 points. Desmond Mason was 3-for-12 and scored eight.

KIRTHMON F. DOZIER

Rasheed Wallace hushes the Bradley Center crowd after scoring in the fourth quarter of Game 4. Wallace scored 20 points in a 109-92 victory. Keith Van Horn is at left.

The Bucks started Keith Van Horn instead of Brian Skinner. But in 36 minutes, Van Horn missed eight of 13 shots. That brought Van Horn's shooting totals to 11-for-38 (28.9 percent) in the series.

Despite the 3-1 advantage, Billups noted that the Pistons vividly remember last season.

"We remember being down, 3-1, to Orlando last year, and they gave us a little momentum and we were able to come back," said Billups, who had nine assists. "We don't want to give them any confidence in Game 5."

THE PLAYOFFS 59

91 PISTONS ROUND 1 GAME 5 SERIES 4-1 BUCKS 77

Milwaukee bucked

Pistons win first-round series, 4-1, await rematch with Jersey

By Mitch Albom

AUBURN HILLS *(APRIL 29, 2004)* — In the NBA, there are players who rise, and players who rise to the occasion, and here was Ben Wallace rising so high to block a Michael Redd jump shot you could drive a tour bus under him. Extending his huge frame as straight as celery, he caught Redd's ball at the peak of its arc and swatted it into next week.

And when he landed — to a mighty Palace roar — even Ben had to admit that was something, and he shook out his frame like a bull after tossing his rider for the last time.

Milwaukee, bucked.

Here is the new thing in the 2004 playoffs, defense that is downright offensive, and the Pistons are registering the patent. The Pistons

Ben Wallace stole the ball from Joe Smith and the Bucks, and the Pistons stole the series with a 91-77 victory in Game 5.

THE THIRD SHIFT 60

needed to control rebounding. Did it. They needed to stifle Milwaukee's scoring threats. Did it. They needed to make the blocks and steals that lead to baskets. Did it.

Milwaukee, bucked.

"We're not getting caught up in the hoopla of it all," said Wallace, who had 12 rebounds and four blocks in the victory that advanced Detroit to the Eastern Conference semifinals. "Experience is on our side."

So are defense, depth and — to keep with the "D-word" theme — dash. Thanks to their stifling defense, the Pistons had 21 fast-break points. You lost count of their lay-ups. You lost count of their dunks. But only after you lost count of their steals, blocks and disruptions. You also lost count of their opponent's air balls.

Milwaukee, bucked.

And no doubt as the Bucks hit the pillows after this game, their nightmares looked a lot like Tayshaun Prince.

"Tayshaun was as consistent as a player could be — over all five games," coach Larry Brown said.

And he's in only his second year.

When Prince wasn't grabbing rebounds (nine) or dishing the ball (eight assists), he was hitting jumpers, or laying it up or dunking to end a break of his own, finishing with 24 points.

Last year, the Pistons fell behind to an inferior Orlando team, three games to one, and had to claw and scrape to escape the first round.

No such problem this time. With the exception of a four-point loss in Game 2, the Pistons were as efficient as the auto part for which they are named.

Milwaukee, bucked.

Now let's see them net New Jersey.

ROMAIN BLANQUART

Tayshaun Prince dunks over Keith Van Horn for two of his 24 points in Game 5. Prince averaged 17.4 points, 7.6 rebounds and 2.2 blocks in the series.

THE PLAYOFFS 61

28 PISTONS ROUND 2 GAME 1 SERIES 1-0 NETS 56

Low-balled

Nets chock-full of holes as Pistons take 1-0 lead

By Drew Sharp

AUBURN HILLS (MAY 3, 2004) — Television sets across America no doubt abandoned the opening salvo of the Pistons-New Jersey second-round playoff series for more captivating fare — like the congressional proceedings on CSPAN.

If the Pistons' opening victory over the Nets is what we can expect for the rest of the series, cover the young ones' eyes.

The Nets missed the league playoff record for fewest points by two. Clearly, that decisive shot went in by accident.

The game brought the fewest combined points in a first half — 62 — in NBA playoff history. And the Nets' 25 first-half points were a franchise-record low. Their triple threat of Jason Kidd, Kenyon

KIRTHMON F. DOZIER

Ben Wallace, left, and New Jersey's Kenyon Martin battle for a loose ball during Game 1 of the Eastern finals at the Palace.

THE THIRD SHIFT 62

Bad blood

There's a lot of history and more than a little mutual dislike between the Pistons and Nets.

The Pistons didn't like that the Nets called a late time-out to set up a relatively meaningless final two points in an 89-71 Detroit victory during their last meeting nearly two months ago. The score denied the Pistons a sixth straight game in which they held the opposition to fewer than 70 points.

The Nets didn't like that the Pistons kept their first unit on the floor against the Jersey scrubs late in the game.

The Pistons said they don't think the Nets were as good as their 4-0 sweep in last year's conference finals suggested.

The Nets said the Pistons were nothing more than whiners.

So saddle up; it's going to be a long ride.

By Drew Sharp

JULIAN H. GONZALEZ

After the Red Wings lost in the second round of the NHL playoffs, Detroit sports fans focused their energy on the Pistons.

Dream denied

While the Pistons won Game 1 against the Nets, the Red Wings' season ended. There would be no Stanley Cup to go with the ones the Red Wings won in 1997, '98 and 2002. Martin Gelinas knocked a loose puck out of the crease and into the net with 46.9 seconds left in overtime, lifting the Calgary Flames to a 1-0 victory at the Saddledome in Calgary, Alberta. The No. 6 Western Conference seed eliminated the top-seeded Wings from the second round of the NHL playoffs in six games.

Martin and Richard Jefferson made only four field goals among them in the first half.

Tayshaun Prince had a strong effort — 15 points, 10 rebounds and five assists. Jefferson, who manhandled Prince in last year's New Jersey sweep of the Pistons, shot 1-for-12 from the field.

New Jersey shot an ice-cold 27.1 percent from the field, making just 19 of 70 shots. Detroit's victory ended a 14-game winning streak for the Nets against Eastern Conference opponents in the playoffs.

The last time these two met, in March, the Nets scrambled to score 70 points. They had difficulty reaching 50 this time.

"It was important for us to get this first win, because nobody had been able to beat these guys in the Eastern Conference the last couple of years," Prince said. "I don't know if we had to prove something to them."

They did.

Respect, as well as baskets, will be hard to earn in this series.

WORKING OVERTIME

■ Near the end of the game, a blond streak flashed off the bench. Like a superhero, Darko Milicic, the human victory cigar, entered the game to loud cheers.

■ Nets guard Jason Kidd: "We were on fire. We were shooting for the lowest score."

■ By the end of the game, Pistons fans were shouting "Byron Scott" at Nets coach Lawrence Frank. Frank replaced Scott, who was fired in January.

KIRTHMON F. DOZIER

Tayshaun Prince gets a rousing ovation from the Palace crowd after he scored and was fouled on a fast break during Game 1 against New Jersey.

THE PLAYOFFS

95 PISTONS ROUND 2 GAME 2 SERIES 2-0 NETS 80

Not half bad

Pistons come on strong in second half

By Mitch Albom

AUBURN HILLS (*MAY 7, 2004*) — In case you didn't recognize this game in the first half, the Pistons lost four of them last May. Four in a row. To this same team. The same way. With New Jersey racing downcourt and stuffing it in their face. With a search party out for a reliable Detroit offense.

By the end of that first half, Detroit had only 34 points and an assortment of bugaboos: technical fouls, traveling calls, even a palming violation.

At the buzzer, as the Nets headed into the tunnel, Kenyon Martin had a smirk on his face that said: "Yep, we knew it. Same old Pistons."

Then the Pistons did something they didn't do last year, maybe couldn't do last year. They took the smirk off Martin's face and wiped the floor with it.

"Everything changed," coach Larry Brown said after the second-half comeback, describing in two words what it took 61 points, 20 rebounds and a choking defense to accomplish.

The Pistons came back from a 12-point deficit to win by 15. This was a night when Detroit's most reliable recent offensive weapon, Tayshaun Prince, didn't make a basket.

Chauncey Billups finished with 28 points and 13 assists, and Richard Hamilton also scored 28 points, shooting 9-for-17 from the field.

The Pistons began the third quarter with that old reliable offensive juggernaut — Ben Wallace. He hit a jumper. Then another. And another.

"I told him to get involved," Brown said sheepishly, "but I didn't tell him to shoot jumpers. He did that on his own."

JULIAN H. GONZALEZ
Forward Richard Jefferson extends for a lay-up against Rasheed Wallace (30) and Ben Wallace in the first quarter. Jefferson made five of 13 shots in Game 2.

THE THIRD SHIFT 64

When told that, Big Ben, who scored all eight of his points in the third quarter, grinned and said, "Hey, if they're gonna leave me open..."

And Rasheed Wallace — well, let's face it. He'll take some shots that'll make you rip your hair out. But when they rip the net — well, it's the opponent that's ripping its hair out. Just ask New Jersey.

"They hit one shot and another and another," Jason Kidd said. "And you look up and suddenly you're down 12."

Funny. Weren't the Pistons saying the same thing about the Nets a year ago?

Hung jury

The perfect symbol for an imperfect product, William Hung spent part of his 15 minutes of celebrity as the off-keynote speaker for Eastern Conference basketball.

"He clangs! He clangs!"

The tone-deaf entertainer of "American Idol" infamy must have sincerely felt at home as the halftime act Friday night at the Palace.

He missed notes like New Jersey has missed shots — with nauseating frequency. But he wasn't alone in not hearing the self-inflicted damage.

NBA commissioner David Stern attended Friday's game, without the need for a blindfold and cigarette.

Of course, some earplugs were necessary to get through halftime.

KIRTHMON F. DOZIER

There were a few sour notes for the Pistons, like "American Idol" reject William Hung's rendition of "She Bangs" during halftime at the Palace.

ROMAIN BLANQUART

Rasheed Wallace celebrates his basket in the fourth quarter of the Pistons' Game 2 victory over the Nets. Wallace had 15 points and three blocks as Detroit took a 2-0 series lead.

THE PLAYOFFS 65

Net-worked

Pistons can't handle Jefferson's 30, let Nets back in series

By Drew Sharp

EAST RUTHERFORD, N.J. *(MAY 9, 2004)* — It's not that the Pistons mind having Ben Wallace as their leading scorer.

It's when he's their only scorer that it's cause for concern.

Only three games old, this series is already notable for its explosive, laughably lopsided scoring runs. But this night, the joke was on the Pistons.

New Jersey opened with a 15-2 run.

Desperation has a way of narrowing your focus and simplifying your purpose. And the Nets figured the faster they ran, the further they could distance themselves from an embarrassing series start in Auburn Hills.

And the Pistons cordially accommodated their hosts.

It was the Nets who benefited from a double-digit breather, cutting the Pistons' series advantage to 2-1.

Tayshaun Prince (four points, no field goals) reverted back to a frog as the man he was supposedly defending, Richard Jefferson, scored a career playoff-high 30 points, making 10 of his first 16 shots and meeting every Pistons comeback with a jump shot or dunk.

Nets coach Lawrence Frank made a defensive adjustment, starting Kerry Kittles on Chauncey Billups and Jason Kidd on Richard Hamilton. The Nets also donned red socks for the first time in the series.

And that meant a red alert for the Pistons. Billups (1-for-10 from the field) and Hamilton (4-for-15) laid enough brick to erect an annex

In a Game 3 loss to the Nets, Tayshaun Prince had the look of, "What's going on?" Prince had no field goals and no rebounds.

to Continental Airlines Arena. Billups had two assists, Hamilton none.

Ben Wallace, who seemed to be the only Piston to recognize the magnitude of the situation, had 15 points, 24 rebounds and four assists.

And Rasheed Wallace?

He went 0-for-5 from behind the arc and was in foul trouble all night.

Eight minutes into the game, the Pistons had five points — and Big Ben was responsible for four.

Yeah, you'd figure that the Nets would like their chances with those percentages.

NETS 94 — ROUND 2 GAME 4 — SERIES 2-2 — PISTONS 79

Comeback Kidd

Struggling Nets star delivers triple-double; series tied

By Jemele Hill

EAST RUTHERFORD, N.J. (MAY 11, 2004) — After Richard Jefferson scored 30 points for the Nets in Game 3, it was point guard Jason Kidd's turn to step it up in Game 4 at Continental Airlines Arena.

Kidd, who had made only nine of 40 shots in the series, came through with 22 points, 11 assists and 10 rebounds in a victory over the Pistons in the Eastern Conference semifinals.

His triple-double allowed the Nets to even the series at two games apiece.

"I called it. He hadn't had a triple-double in the series. He was due for one," Jefferson said. "J-Kidd is not going to shy away from a challenge. Sooner or later, those shots are going to fall."

A series that started off with so much potential has suddenly become a dogfight for the Pistons, who squandered a 2-0 series lead.

The Nets, who led by as many as 23, outrebounded Detroit, 49-33, and outscored the Pistons, 40-22, in the paint. Those rebounds contributed directly to their 25-11 advantage in fast-break points. Jefferson had 19 points and Kenyon Martin added 16 points and 15 rebounds.

And the Pistons couldn't do much about it. They were a one-man show on the offensive end, with Richard Hamilton scoring 30 points. Hamilton, the only Piston who had a field goal in the third quarter, was the only Piston in double figures.

Chauncey Billups played only 27 minutes because of back spasms, scoring six points on 2-of-7 shooting. Rasheed Wallace's sore left foot flared and he was limping in the second quarter. He finished the game, but he scored six points and was 1-of-5 from the field.

"If (they) were healthy it wouldn't have mattered tonight," coach Larry Brown said.

ROMAIN BLANQUART

Richard Jefferson hugs teammate Jason Kidd in the third quarter of Game 4. Kidd had 22 points, 11 assists and 10 rebounds.

Larry vs. Lawrence

The saga between New Jersey coach Lawrence Frank and Larry Brown continued throughout the series.

Brown commented that Frank's hiring showed that "anybody" could coach in the NBA. Brown and former Nets coach Byron Scott, who was fired despite back-to-back appearances in the NBA Finals, have a close relationship.

Nets president Rod Thorn on Brown: "Way off base. Lawrence has put in his time. ... That's bush."

THE PLAYOFFS

127 NETS ROUND 2 GAME 5 SERIES 2-3 3OT PISTONS 120

Sooo Long?

Pistons' season could end in Game 6 at New Jersey

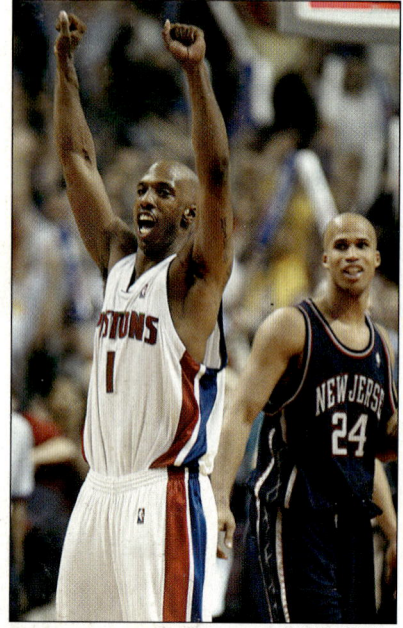

Detroit's Chauncey Billups, who scored 31 points, celebrates his three-pointer from near half-court that forced the first overtime. The shot went in off the backboard at the buzzer. Richard Jefferson is at right.

By Mitch Albom

AUBURN HILLS *(MAY 14, 2004)* — He should have been the hero. Chauncey Billups should be doing interviews about the miracle shot, how he knew all along that it was going in, how he practiced that shot when he was a kid, how he dreamed it just the way it happened in the final second of regulation of a crucial Game 5, just inside the half-court line, launched like a prayer, kissing the glass in a frame of red light and banking in for a tie game to force overtime.

He should have been the hero — and the Pistons should be celebrating a victory inspired by that most unlikely of three-pointers. Instead, they are facing a Herculean challenge, going home for the season unless they win two from a New Jersey team that has beaten them three straight.

Final score, 127-120, in a triple-overtime, four-hour-plus evening sure to be remembered as a classic by everyone else, and as classic heartburn for Pistons fans. For here is the killer: Billups made the most unlikely shot of the night, but he couldn't make enough of the normal ones — while a big, chunky red-headed bench player named Brian Scalabrine (I know, "Who?"), a guy who was averaging 2.2 points in these playoffs, did what Billups and the rest of the Pistons couldn't do: made shots when they counted.

Four-for-four? Six of seven shots total? Seventeen points? Brian Scalabrine?

Yep. And every one seemed to be

Larry Brown watches his team with a nervous look in the first quarter of Game 5 — a triple-overtime loss to the Nets. "I'm proud just to be a part of a game like that," Brown said.

THE THIRD SHIFT 68

Many Pistons fans were on the edge of their seats during the triple-overtime thriller. Clockwise from right, Jeff Kawa, 26; Marcus Zakrzewski, 26; Chris Sample, 25, and George Cronin, 26, watch the game at Cronin's Berkley home.

a dagger.

"I thought this game went six overtimes," Scalabrine said when it was over. "We just happened to make a few more big shots."

Brian Scalabrine? Not Kenyon Martin? Not Jason Kidd? Nope. Those guys were fairly neutralized. Brian Scalabrine?

Yes, especially his final three-pointer with 44 seconds left in the third overtime — and just two seconds left on the shot clock.

"I'm tired," Billups said after playing 55 exhausting minutes. "But a game like this is tough to lose. It just seemed like every time they needed a big shot, they knocked one down."

It's true. The Nets made nearly half of their 24 three-point attempts. Billups heaved up 29 shots. He made only nine.

Oh, sure, he wasn't the only one. Lindsey Hunter had chances in the second overtime but missed open three-point tries and finished 0-for-5. Mehmet Okur was a non-factor, making one of three. Tayshaun Prince, who started hot, finished 5-for-15. And Richard Hamilton fouled out in regulation with 11 points — if you can remember back that far.

The Pistons endured stretches of futility, missing their last 11 attempts in regulation before that miracle by Chauncey.

They shot 38 percent, at home. They made only six of their 25 three-point attempts. And they missed 12 of 42 free throws.

Was it an amazing game? Sure. There were 24 lead changes, 21 ties, and the Pistons took 111 field goal attempts to 86 for the Nets.

A battle. A marathon. An exhausting night. By the end, a playoff-record eight players fouled out. Heck, it was easier to say who was still eligible. I don't want to use that tired phrase "a war of attrition," but Isiah Thomas was sitting courtside and you know, they still have his uniform somewhere. . . .

The Pistons could have used his shooting, that was for sure.

No coach is perfect

Game 5 showed it. Larry Brown inexplicably went with an overtime lineup of Chauncey Billups, Lindsey Hunter, Mike James, Darvin Ham and Tayshaun Prince, while Mehmet Okur sat on the bench. The Pistons' offense floundered, and Brown was heavily criticized for the move. Brown put in Okur for longer stretches in Game 6.

THE PLAYOFFS 69

PISTONS 81 ROUND 2 GAME 6 SERIES 3-3 NETS 75

Rip, tied

Not quitting time: Hamilton's late jumper forces Game 7

By Mitch Albom

EAST RUTHERFORD, N.J. *(MAY 16, 2004)* — The final buzzer sounded, and the Pistons hugged in the eerie silence of a disappointed crowd. Or maybe they were just holding each other up.

"If there was ever a doubt about this team's heart," Pistons president Joe Dumars said, "they answered it tonight."

Dumars looked tired. And he didn't even play.

The Pistons have a Game 7 on their schedule, after showing moxie in this crucial Game 6, going into the dark hole of the Jersey swamps and swimming away with a wrenching victory.

"We said before this started, it's gonna be a grind," said Richard Hamilton, who scored 24 points and the clinching jump shot with 15.5 seconds left.

New Jersey was threatening to become the mental roadblock to these Pistons that the Boston Celtics once were to the Bad Boys. A loss would have meant back-to-back playoffs in which the Nets won four in a row.

But the Pistons won the first game they absolutely had to win this postseason, in an unfriendly building, after a haunting triple-overtime loss less than 48 hours earlier. They came back from a dismal start in which they missed eight of their first nine shots, and they came back from a brutal third quarter in which they missed seven of their first eight shots.

Then Hamilton hit a jumper. Then a lay-up. Then another lay-up. The Pistons crawled back in, then ran way ahead. By halftime, the Pistons had a 14-point lead. On the road?

Yes. And then they nearly squandered the whole thing. They came out of the locker room flat as warm

Ben Wallace goes in for a lay-up between Kenyon Martin, left, and Richard Jefferson. Wallace had six points and 20 rebounds in Game 6.

KIRTHMON F. DOZIER

soda. They scored 10 points in 12 minutes.

But when the fourth quarter started, Mehmet Okur came alive just in time, grabbing crucial rebounds. Lindsey Hunter hit a huge three-pointer. Corliss Williamson played tough.

Finally, with 15.5 seconds left, Hamilton hit his 18-foot jumper over Jason Kidd that put the game away.

"That's one of those shots you dream about as a kid," Hamilton said. "I mean, that's what you play for."

That, and this: that last buzzer, a few sweaty hugs and the sweet silence of an unhappy crowd.

THE THIRD SHIFT 70

PISTONS 90 ROUND 2 GAME 7 SERIES 4-3 NETS 69

Hair we go!

Pistons, Big Ben tell Nets to 'Fro-gedaboutit, advance to meet Pacers

By Mitch Albom

AUBURN HILLS *(MAY 20, 2004)* — Ben Wallace wore his hair in an Afro, and when a man's hair rises, can the man do any less? So Wallace stood up, nearly taking the game over, and Rasheed Wallace, bad foot and all, stood up, too, and Rip Hamilton stood up, and Chauncey Billups stood up. They all stood up and stared into the snarling dragon of this Game 7, then they dropped baskets down its throat until it choked.

Nets, clipped. Final score, 90-69. A series that was like a college course in perseverance, is finally, blissfully, over. What the Nets taught the Pistons last season they learned well. You can't let those guys run, you must squeeze Jason Kidd.

Done and done. The Pistons squashed the Nets into terrible 36-percent shooting and 16 poisonous turnovers. Kidd was blanked, while Billups scored 22.

No more Kenyon, no more Kidd, don't care what Scalabrine did!

Ben Wallace was insane. Just when you think you've seen it all, he morphs into a shooting guard. He hit eight of his first nine shots, including many outside jumpers. He finished with 18 points, in addition to his rebounds and defense.

"It was Game 7," he said afterward in the press area, holding his baby son on his lap. "If we were gonna go down, we were gonna go down swinging."

The Palace? It was wild. Loud? It was deafening. It was a blurry mass of ThunderStix. This is what home-court advantage is supposed to sound like, folks.

For some reason, this win resonated much larger. Perhaps because after a decade as Hockeytown, Detroit was rediscovering its addiction to basketball.

These Pistons are growing up before our eyes.

Ben Wallace drives by New Jersey's Rodney Rogers. Wallace scored 18 points in Game 7, many on jumpers. He shot 8-for-10 from the field. — KIRTHMON F. DOZIER

A long layoff

The Nets-Pistons series took a whopping 18 days for seven games. There were four-day layoffs between Games 1 and 2, and Games 6 and 7.

From Fox Sport Net's "Best Damn Sports Show Period" funnyman Tom Arnold's bit: "Things You Would Never Say to the New Jersey Nets":

■ "Hey, Nets, forget Ben Wallace. Your sorry (butts) couldn't handle Mike Wallace."
■ "Hey, Nets, you've got Richard Jefferson playing more like Weezie Jefferson."
■ "Hey, Nets, thank God for 'The Sopranos.' At least somebody in New Jersey has a decent shooting percentage."

THE PLAYOFFS 71

Face-off

An awkward reunion in Indy

JULIAN H. GONZALEZ

Indiana coach Rick Carlisle didn't have an air of bitterness entering the Eastern Conference finals against his former team. "My memory is very selective short-term memory. I choose to remember the good things about my time in Detroit."

By Mitch Albom and Perry A. Farrell

A day before the biggest series in the Eastern Conference, which features more subplots than a week-long airing of "General Hospital," Ben Wallace was asked whether he missed Rick Carlisle, the coach who guided the Pistons to 100 victories over the previous two seasons and a trip to the Eastern Conference finals.

Understand, the question was from a television reporter new to the scene and probably not wise to the ways of the tell-it-like-it-is Wallace.

In typical fashion, Wallace looked at the reporter and said, "I don't miss nobody. Why would I miss him?"

When asked whether any of his teammates missed Carlisle, Wallace's reply was simple: "No, this is a business."

Wallace's teammates said they didn't have a problem with Carlisle, and they communicated with him when necessary. But when the organization decided to fire Carlisle and hire Larry Brown last June, there was no outcry.

Last year around this time, Carlisle and the Pistons had just defeated Brown and the 76ers to advance to the conference finals, and Carlisle and president Joe Dumars were side by side laughing and slapping each other in congratulations. It seemed like their future together was bright.

A few days later, the Pistons were out of the playoffs. And Carlisle was out of a job.

"It was crystal clear to me that they wanted Larry Brown," Carlisle says now. "I was told in the conver-

THE THIRD SHIFT 72

sation when they let me go that they were going to hire him. And I understand that. He's the best of the best."

Maybe. But Carlisle did beat Brown's team the last time they met in the playoffs.

Then came rumors that Carlisle was somehow too aloof, that he had alienated certain players and offended certain staff members.

Carlisle, 44, did a fine job with the team when he was here. And Brown, 63, has done an equally fine job in his first season at the helm. This might be one of those rare times where everybody benefited, even if Carlisle had to bleed a little.

"As for this series, I'm not sure it should ever be about the coaches," Carlisle says. "It's about the players. It's a players' league, and I'll do my best to get my guys prepared, and Larry will do the same. I'm not sure it's much beyond that."

Carlisle will say that phrase a lot. "It's not much beyond that." He is a guy who looks to diffuse rather than inflate. He is a cerebral, focused, genial man, who might not be perfect for every player in the league, but let's not forget, Brown and Allen Iverson weren't exactly Burns and Allen.

So can you go home again? And what makes it "home?" Those questions will echo in this series. Pacers fans admit their franchise was nowhere until Brown turned it in the right direction. Then he left. Now he returns. Pistons fans know Carlisle must be credited with a similar turn of the chains in Detroit. Then he was canned. Now he returns.

It's a horse race, basically, only certain jockeys have jumped saddles. But Carlisle might understand better how you leave things behind. His legacy is on both sides of the basketball, as is Brown's. And when they toss it up, there'll be a lot of invisible hands trying to tip that thing their way.

Most of the Pistons said they enjoyed the freedom Larry Brown gave them compared to Rick Carlisle's strict play-calling.

Different under Brown

When the Pistons fired Rick Carlisle in 2003 and hired Larry Brown, they replaced one of their best coaches with another. But Carlisle and Brown approach the job in different ways:

Style: Think of Carlisle as the architect of a skyscraper, designing every piece in the most efficient, orderly and functional way, down to the last ashtray. Think of Brown as the designer of a botanical garden, planting flowers here and bushes there and trees over there, watching how they interact, understanding that the whole scheme is always changing.

System: Carlisle stood by his system; Brown constantly fiddles. With Carlisle, players knew how much they'd play; Brown's playing rotation varies by the game. Carlisle preferred a half-court game, where his players ran his offense as he saw fit; Brown likes to cause disorder with his defense, giving the Pistons the freedom to create in the open court. Carlisle called a ton of plays; Brown calls some but is more likely to let players figure things out.

Run: The Pistons run more under Brown and hit the offensive glass. If more players try for offensive rebounds, that means fewer players get back on defense to stop the fast break. Carlisle never wanted to get into a run-and-gun game. Brown wants to run, and he loves second-chance hoops.

Everyone shoot: Brown made an adjustment that, on the surface, seems odd. He has asked one of his best scorers, Chauncey Billups, to shoot less, and asked one of his least effective scorers, Ben Wallace, to shoot more. Why? Because Brown has an unyielding belief that basketball is the ultimate team game. Every player can contribute — and by doing so, he makes it easier for everybody else.

— By Michael Rosenberg

THE PLAYOFFS 73

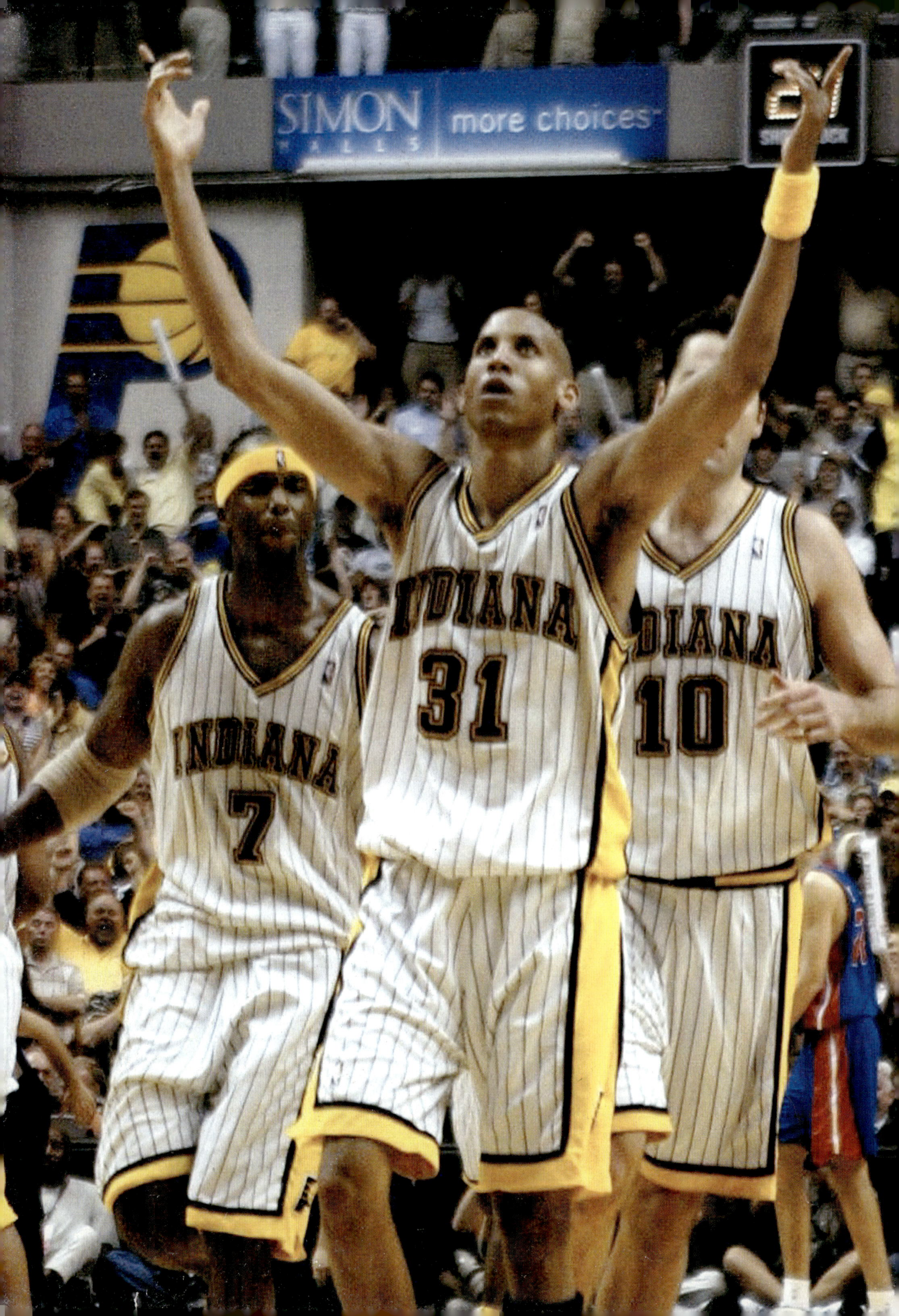
SIMON
more choices
INDIANA
31
10
7

`[ 78 ] PACERS  ROUND 3  GAME 1  SERIES 0-1  PISTONS [ 74 ]`

Miller time

Reggie's only triple sinks Pistons, gives Pacers early lead

By Perry A. Farrell

INDIANAPOLIS (MAY 22, 2004) — Not a go-to guy anymore but always a threat, Reggie Miller delivered the first blow in the series. He nailed a three-pointer with 31.7 seconds left, breaking a 74-all tie and sending the Pacers to a 78-74 victory in Game 1 of the Eastern Conference finals.

Miller sealed the game by scoring the last four points for the Pacers after being badly outplayed by Richard Hamilton, who led all scorers with 23. The three was Miller's only field goal.

The Pistons had just one field goal in the final 7:45 — a triple by Tayshaun Prince with 1:40 left.

"It was the kind of game everybody expected, intense and not really high-scoring," said Pacers coach Rick Carlisle. "When they went up by two on the Prince shot it was gut-check time.

"The thing about Reggie, as games get tighter he's the kind of guy that focuses in even more. It was certainly time because we were having troubles."

Jermaine O'Neal had 21 points and 14 rebounds, leading four Pacers in double figures, while Ben Wallace had 11 points, 22 rebounds, five blocked shots and five assists for Detroit.

"We missed some opportunities," said Chauncey Billups. "I can look back on it now and remember a couple of plays that I would've done different."

Said Wallace: "We made a lot of silly plays at the end. One shot didn't beat us. We took quick shots and didn't play smart. We can't jack up quick threes and expect to win the game. We tried to be the one to win it, instead of making plays for our teammates. Reggie's been doing that for years."

KIRTHMON F. DOZIER

Rasheed Wallace defends against Jermaine O'Neal during the fourth quarter of Game 1 of the conference finals against Indiana. O'Neal scored 21 points in the Pacer victory.

Photo on previous page by JULIAN H. GONZALEZ
Pacers veteran guard Reggie Miller celebrates another crucial three-pointer. This one, with 31 seconds left, just about sealed the Pistons' fate in Game 1.

THE PLAYOFFS 75

Guaransheed!

It's put up or shut up for Pistons after Wallace's bold prediction

By Perry A. Farrell

INDIANAPOLIS — As soon as Rasheed Wallace entered the Pacers' practice facility, he was swarmed by every member of the media in one moving mass of cameras, tape recorders and notepads.

Everyone wanted to know whether Wallace would back off his bold comments.

Moments after the Pistons' 78-74 Game 1 loss to the Pacers, Wallace declared: "I'm guaranteeing Game 2. That's the bottom line. That's all I'm saying. They will not win Game 2. You heard that from me. Y'all can print whatever you want. Put it on the front page, back page, middle of the page. They will not win Game 2."

Surely, a day later Wallace would backtrack — at least a little — especially after hanging out with Indiana star Jermaine O'Neal, his friend since their days with Portland.

Nope.

"I said it last night, and I'm saying it again: We will win Game 2," Wallace said. "I'm not trying to sound ignorant or anything, but we will win. Nothing's changed. We're winning Game 2, just like I said last night."

Wallace scored just four points on 1-for-7 shooting, with five fouls and seven rebounds in 36 frustrating minutes in Game 1.

"Knowing him, he feels responsible for the game last night," coach Larry Brown said.

Whether a confidence builder for the Pistons or locker-room fodder for the Pacers, Wallace's guarantee placed the spotlight on him and away from his teammates.

JULIAN H. GONZALEZ

Detroit forward Rasheed Wallace is surrounded by microphones as he enters practice May 23 in Indianapolis. He repeated his guarantee that the Pistons would win Game 2.

'Sheed reactions

THE PACERS SAY . . .

How the Indiana Pacers reacted to Rasheed Wallace's guarantee of a Detroit victory in Game 2:

Reggie Miller: "I really don't know what's in Rasheed's head."

Ron Artest: "A lot of guys talk in the world. This is just another guy talking in the world."

Benchwarmer Scot Pollard: "I guarantee that there's going to be a Game 2, and that someone's going to win it. And I guarantee that Rasheed will probably be in the game and I won't."

THE PISTONS SAY . . .

Corliss Williamson: "It's our job as teammates to rally around him and make sure he's right."

Chauncey Billups: "I got his back, baby. I'm not mad at him at all."

Larry Brown: "It ain't about Rasheed only; it's about all of us. We got to get it done."

THAT G-WORD AGAIN

Some of our favorite guarantees:

Lomas Brown: Former Lion guaranteed a playoff victory at Philadelphia in 1995. The Lions fell behind, 51-7, and lost, 58-37.

David Boston (1997) and Terry Glenn (1995): Ohio State receivers guaranteed victories over U-M. The Wolverines won both games.

Jim Harbaugh: U-M QB guaranteed a victory over OSU in 1986. Michigan won, 26-24, at Columbus and went to the Rose Bowl.

Domino's: Former owner Tom Monaghan, also a former Tigers owner, guaranteed pizza delivery in 30 minutes or less. Tigers owner Mike Ilitch guarantees 30 games under .500 by July.

Detroit Medical Center: Promises emergency room patients will be seen by a doctor in 29 minutes or less. Anyone not seen by then gets Tigers tickets.

THE THIRD SHIFT

72 PISTONS ROUND 2 GAME 2 SERIES 1-1 PACERS 67

Prince valiant

Enough said! Amazing block fulfills Rasheed's Game 2 guarantee

The man who guaranteed a Detroit win in Game 2 — Rasheed Wallace — yells to the crowd after the Pistons backed it up May 24 at Conseco Fieldhouse.

KIRTHMON F. DOZIER

By Mitch Albom

INDIANAPOLIS *(MAY 24, 2004)* — Hey, all he said was they would win. He didn't say it would be pretty. Just because Rasheed Wallace missed his first shot, his second, third and fourth shots, his fifth and sixth shots, made his seventh, then missed his eighth and ninth, then threw up an air ball with his 10th, hey, that doesn't mean he was wrong about guaranteeing a victory, does it?

What counts is the score, not the score settled. On a night of forgettable shooting, the best plays were blocks, and the best block of all came with 17 seconds left with Indiana's Reggie Miller, the star of Game 1, heading to the hoop with a stolen ball for the tying lay-up in Game 2.

And then came Tayshaun Prince, flying higher than ever as a Piston, and he slapped that ball away and landed into the photographers.

And suddenly, Wallace was right.

And he owes Prince a thank-you.

"One of the greatest hustle plays I've ever seen," coach Larry Brown would call it.

"When I saw Tayshaun chasing Reggie," Rip Hamilton would add, "I said to myself, 'Reggie better dunk it, or Tay's gonna get it.' "

He got it. Pistons win, 72-67.

The Pistons almost blew another fourth-quarter lead — before Prince, running with his head down

THE PLAYOFFS 77

BLOCK PARTY

The Pistons blocked 19 shots in Game 2, one shy of the NBA playoff record.

Pistons who blocked shots:

Rasheed Wallace	5
Tayshaun Prince	4
Ben Wallace	4
Elden Campbell	3
Chauncey Billups	1
Mehmet Okur	1
Corliss Williamson	1

Pacers whose shots got blocked:

Ron Artest	7
Al Harrington	4
Jermaine O'Neal	3
Austin Croshere	2
Jonathan Bender	1
Jeff Foster	1
Reggie Miller	1

HOOSIER MASCOT?

What is a Pacer, anyway? According to team lore, the name is supposed to represent Indiana's racing tradition — both the Indianapolis 500 pace car and harness racing.

---

like an Olympic sprinter, then rising at just the right angle, caught the ball but not Miller, and stuffed a sock in the Indiana crowd.

A few free throws later, the series was tied, 1-1. Home-court advantage shifted to the Pistons.

They won because Prince has been doing a great defensive job on Ron Artest — who was again abysmal (5-for-21). And because Rasheed at least partly made up for his shooting with his defense on Jermaine O'Neal, who didn't score in the second half.

They won because Hamilton continues to be their only reliable offense, and they won because of those 19 blocks (a franchise playoff record). And, yes, they won because Indiana shot terribly — 28 percent, after shooting 34 percent in Game 1.

Rasheed Wallace took his time coming out of the trainer's room with a strange sense of entitlement for a guy who shot 4-for-19.

"So y'all want to get up in my face now," he said, finally.

"Do you have any other guarantees?" he was asked.

Ben Wallace draws the foul while going inside against Jermaine O'Neal in the fourth quarter of Game 2 in Indianapolis. Detroit won, 72-67.

"Yeah. I guarantee Games 3 and 4 will be in Detroit."

Well. Can you blame him for turning shy? This was not exactly a sure thing until those final moments. And had Detroit lost, everyone would be asking about Rasheed's miserable offense.

But because Detroit won, reporters hovered as if he were a soothsayer. You can't blame the media for hyping this. What else are we going to focus on in this series — the great shooting?

The Pacers scored 24 points in the second half. The Pistons had an amazing 19 blocks and an embarrassing 23 baskets.

And Rasheed Wallace had about as bad a game as a prognosticator could have. Imagine Joe Namath in that Super Bowl with a 4-for-19 passing day.

But Wallace didn't seem bothered. When the fans hooted and hollered, he encouraged them to be louder. He raised his arms as if to say, "More, more." They obliged.

If Rasheed wanted extra attention to motivate himself, he got it.

Then again, he got the victory, too.

Photo on following page by KIRTHMON F. DOZIER

Tayshaun Prince makes the game-saving block of Reggie Miller's shot. Prince raced down the court, blocked the ball, kept it inbounds, and the Pistons pulled out the Game 2 victory.

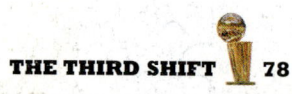

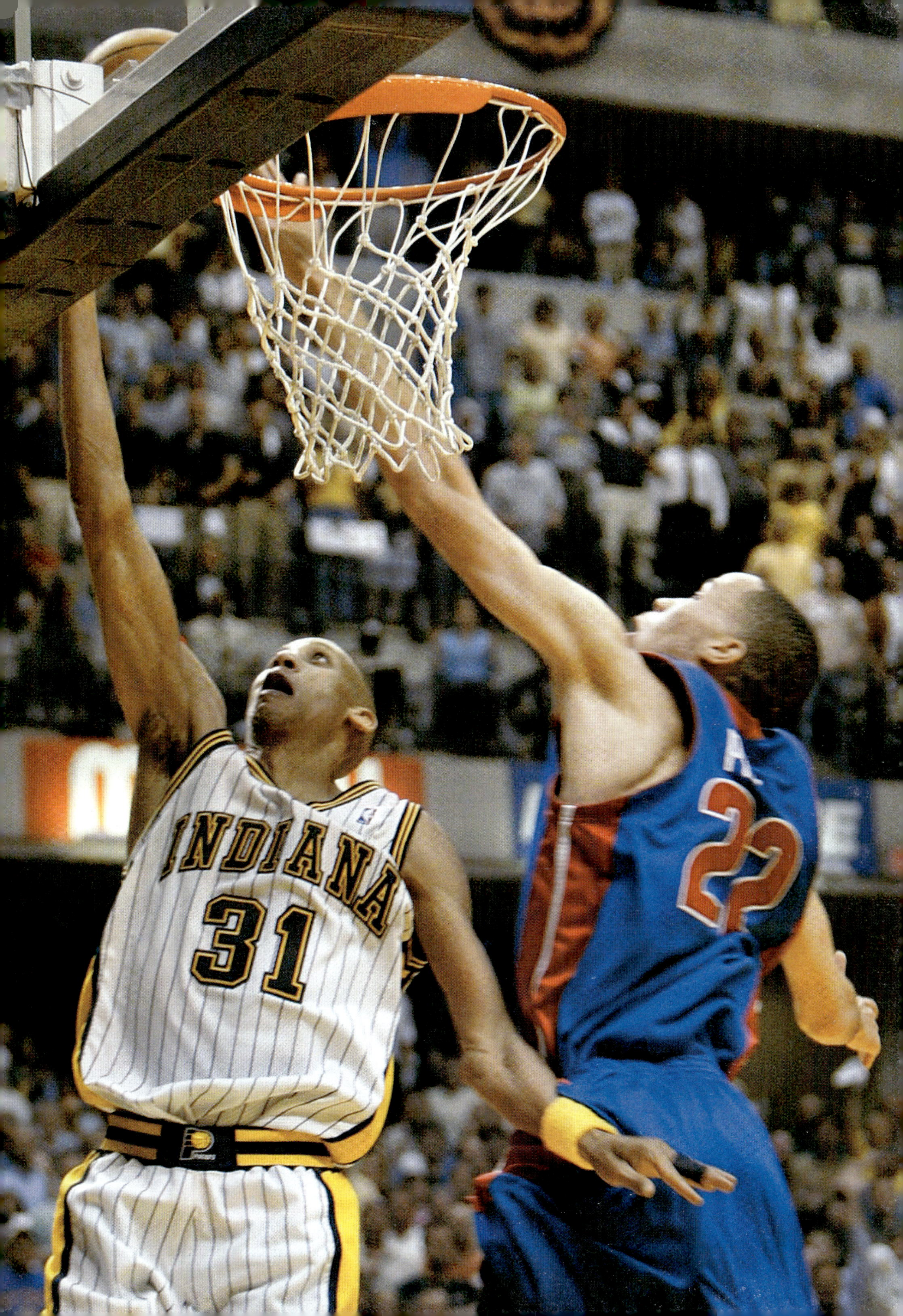
INDIANA
31
22

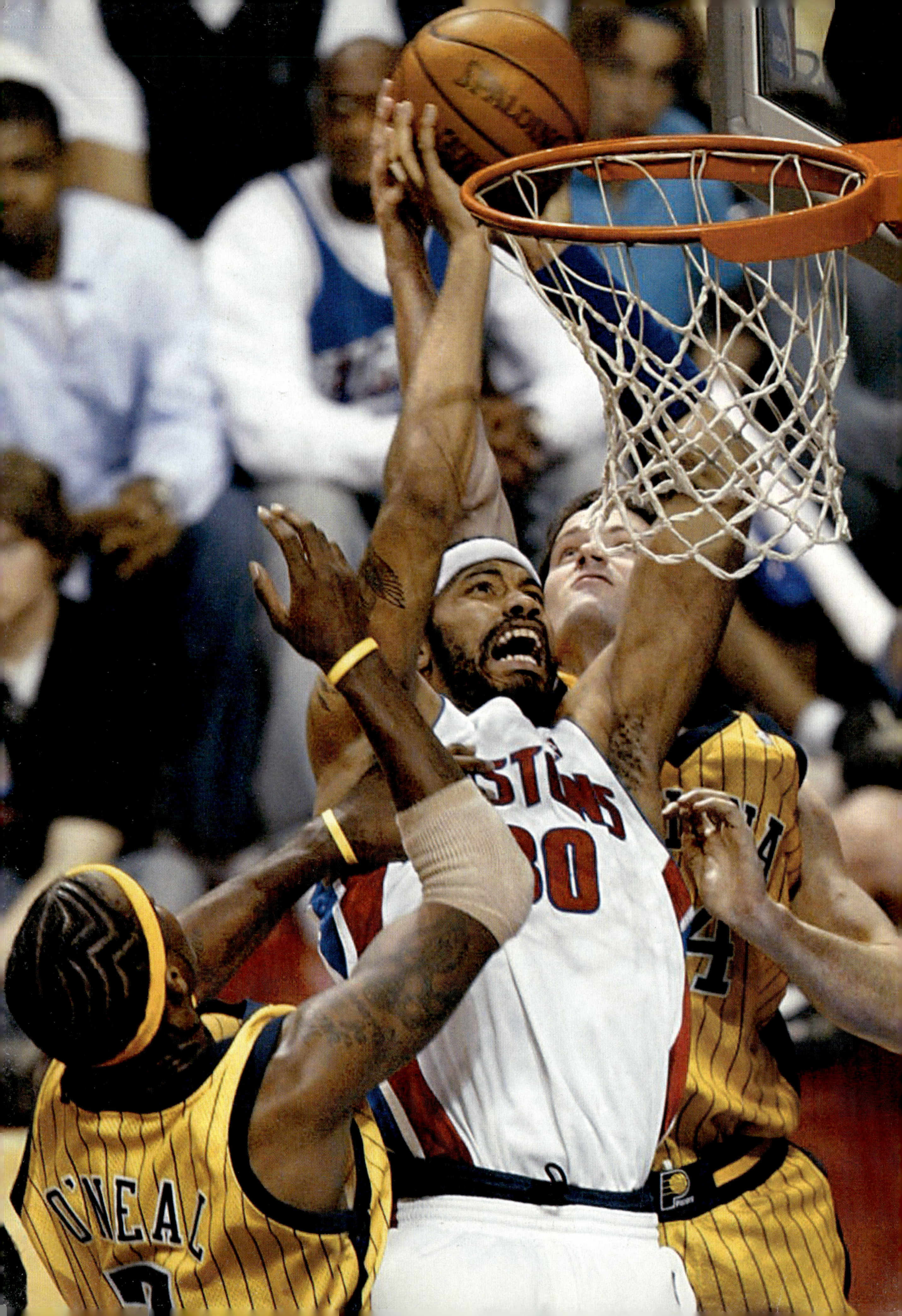
O'NEAL

85 PISTONS ROUND 3 GAME 3 SERIES 2-1 PACERS 78

Good 'n' ugly

Wallace X2 combination stands tall as Pistons take 2-1 lead

Ben Wallace goes up and over Jermaine O'Neal during the second half of Game 3 of the Eastern finals. Wallace grabbed 16 rebounds and scored 17 points.

JULIAN H. GONZALEZ

By Perry A. Farrell

AUBURN HILLS (MAY 26, 2004) — Ben Wallace, co-captain and leader of the Pistons' Wallace X2 combination, didn't disappoint the home crowd in Game 3 of the Eastern Conference finals.

Wallace had 17 points, 16 rebounds and three blocked shots, and the Pistons beat the Indiana Pacers, 85-78, before a sellout crowd of 22,076 at the Palace.

The victory gave the Pistons a 2-1 series lead.

Rasheed Wallace converted a crucial three-point play with the Pacers down one and rallying, and Ben Wallace tipped in a Rasheed miss with 31.6 seconds left.

That gave the Pistons an 82-78 lead and Indiana never scored again.

As the final buzzer sounded, Pacers guard Reggie Miller kicked the ball into the stands. Miller had scored only three points.

"It feels good to score 17 and get the win," Ben Wallace said. "It doesn't matter if I score five or six as long as we win."

Rasheed Wallace's basket came after the Pacers scored 10 straight points to cut the Pistons' lead to 76-75.

"We got the ball inside finally and came up with a three-point play," coach Larry Brown said of the basket with 1:32 left. "Then we made some unbelievable plays. We made a couple of blocks, came up with a couple of loose balls and that was the difference in the game.

"We were fortunate to win, but that's the way all three games have been. I thought our inside people played great."

In a series of poor shooting, Ben Wallace ran against form. He missed only two shots — one from the field, one from the line. He shot 7-for-8 from the field and 3-for-4 from the line.

Rasheed Wallace scored 20 points on 8-for-15 shooting, and Richard Hamilton scored 20 as a team finally scored 80 points in the series.

The Pistons shot 44.1 percent from the field, the Pacers 34.7, their fourth straight game below 35 percent.

It was the third straight tight finish of the series.

OFF THE PACE

The Pacers shot less than 35 percent for the fourth straight game. Their stats the past four games:

GM	OPPONENT	FG	FG%	SCORE
6	Miami	22-68	32.4	W, 73-70
1	Detroit	28-83	33.7	W, 78-74
2	Detroit	22-80	27.5	L, 72-67
3	Detroit	25-72	34.7	L, 85-78

Photo on previous page by MANDI WRIGHT
Detroit's Rasheed Wallace goes to the basket against Pacers Jermaine O'Neal and Austin Croshere in the second quarter of Game 3. Wallace scored 20 points.

THE PLAYOFFS

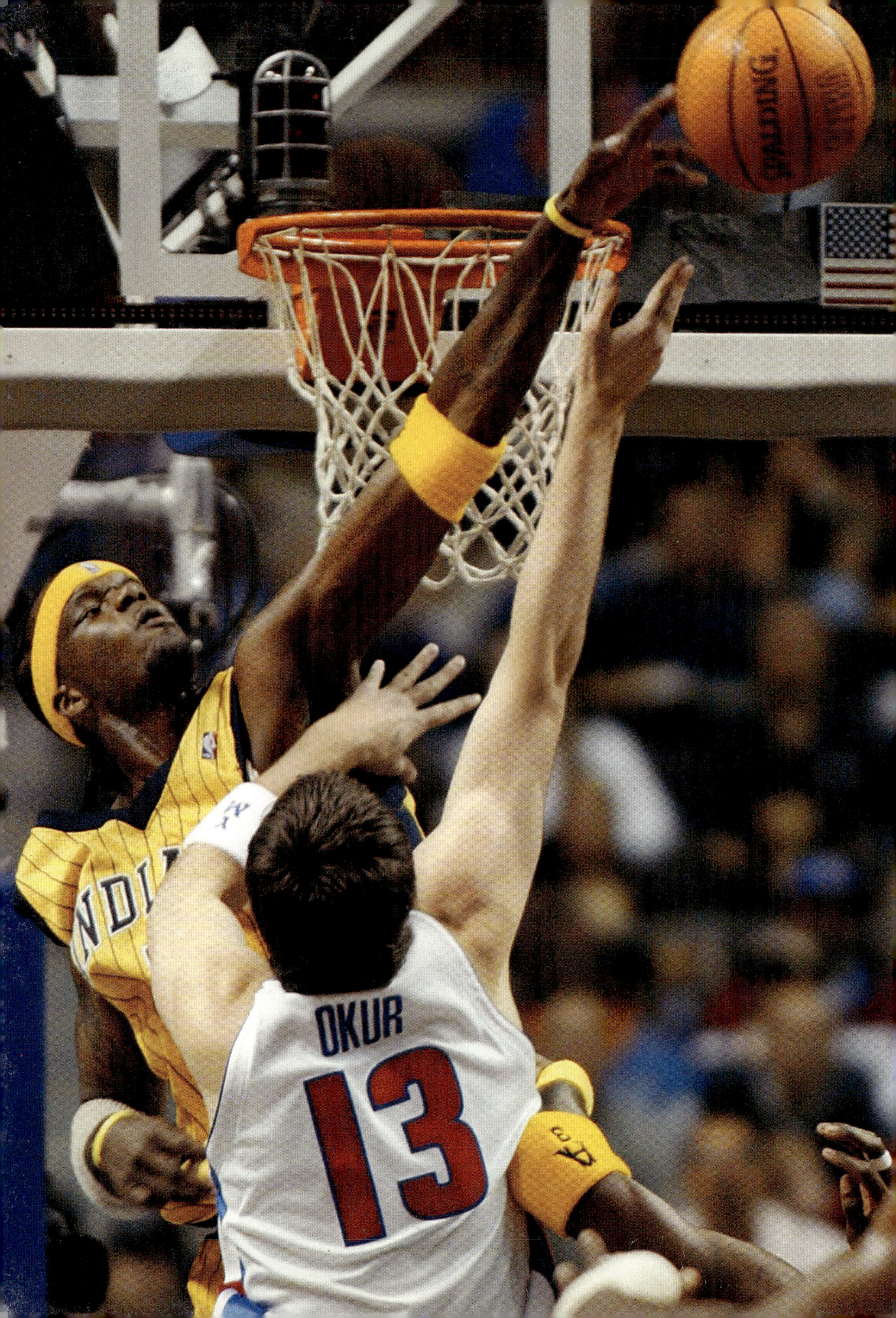
OKUR
13

PACERS 83 ROUND 3 GAME 4 SERIES 2-2 PISTONS 68

Indy-fensible

Pistons lose home-court advantage as hot-shooting Pacers even series

KIRTHMON F. DOZIER

From left, Pistons Tayshaun Prince, Chauncey Billups and Mehmet Okur watch Indiana build a third-quarter lead in Game 4 on May 28 in Auburn Hills. Detroit shot a dismal 30.8 percent as the Pacers evened the series at 2.

By Perry A. Farrell

AUBURN HILLS (MAY 28, 2004) — The Pacers took action. Then they took back home-court advantage.

On Thursday, Indiana had a long practice of film-watching and shooting. On Friday, coach Rick Carlisle inserted Austin Croshere into the starting lineup.

The moves helped put the Pacers back in contention of their Eastern Conference finals series with the Pistons, as they regained home-court advantage with an 83-68 victory in Game 4 at the Palace.

Indiana evened the series, 2-2. In a series of close battles, Game 4 was by far the easiest victory on either side.

"They were better prepared, better coached, and I have to do a better job," coach Larry Brown said. "I look at this game — I'm going to stick my head in the sand. They had the best road record, the best record in the league. We can't play any worse than tonight. Maybe they had a lot to do with it. We couldn't guard anybody out front. We have to do a better job of

Carlisle: Pressure is on Pistons

Rick Carlisle said there's no pressure on his team to advance to the NBA Finals because the Pistons are supposed to make it there or risk a failed season.

"Their whole season is made or broken on whether or not they make it to the Finals," said Carlisle. "They've been here last year. I told our guys before the game that there aren't many people on our bandwagon right now."

INJURY SCARE

Indiana got a huge scare in the first quarter when Jermaine O'Neal suffered a sprained left knee in a scary fall while battling under the boards with Ben Wallace. O'Neal returned to the game. Point guard Jamaal Tinsley missed most of the second half because of injuries. Both struggled with the ailments for the rest of the series.

Photo on previous page by KIRTHMON F. DOZIER

Indiana's 6-foot-11 Jermaine O'Neal blocks the shot of Detroit's 6-11 Mehmet Okur during the Pacers' 83-68 romp in Game 4 of the Eastern Conference finals at the Palace.

JULIAN H. GONZALEZ

Indiana's Al Harrington goes up for the shot in front of Detroit's Corliss Williamson during the second half of Game 4.

defending. We can do it. We've done it before."

Carlisle started Croshere in the frontcourt in place of Jeff Foster. Croshere, who hasn't started in more than two years, entered the game averaging 3.5 points in the playoffs. But the power forward responded with 14 points and three three-pointers.

"I think Austin is a positive for us," teammate Ron Artest said. "If they double off him, he can make shots."

And Croshere made shots — along with the rest of the Pacers.

Indiana shot 45.7 percent from the field after shooting less than 35 percent in each of the first three games. The Pacers also shot 50 percent from three-point land, hitting eight triples.

Artest had his best shooting game of the series, going 8-for-19 with 20 points and 10 rebounds. Jermaine O'Neal also had a double-double with 12 points and 13 rebounds.

KIRTHMON F. DOZIER

Ben Wallace and Elden Campbell make double trouble for Al Harrington in Game 4. But the Pistons were flat on offense in an 83-68 loss at the Palace.

Reggie Miller added 15 points.

Richard Hamilton scored 22 and Chauncey Billups 21 — 12 in the fourth quarter — for the Pistons.

The Pistons shot 30.8 percent.

THE THIRD SHIFT 84

PISTONS 69 | ROUND 3 GAME 5 | SERIES 3-2 | PACERS 65

Rip storm

Hamilton's 33 lifts Pistons to 3-2 lead over Pacers

By Perry A. Farrell

INDIANAPOLIS *(MAY 30, 2004)* — The day started with a tornado touching down about four miles from Conseco Fieldhouse. The Indianapolis 500 was shortened by rain. And Pistons fans were louder than Pacers fans in the arena, donning wigs, signs and throwback jerseys.

A weird day ended with a normal occurrence. Richard Hamilton again torched the Pacers — this time for 33 points in the Pistons' 83-65 Game 5 victory.

"I've never been on the road and had that much fan support before," said Corliss Williamson, who scored five points off the bench. "At times it sounded like a home game. Those are true Piston fans."

The Pistons beat the Pacers on their floor for the second straight time and took a 3-2 series lead.

Hamilton scored his career playoff high on 12-for-22 shooting. Rasheed Wallace provided eight of his 22 points in the fourth quarter and finished 8-for-17 from the field.

Detroit held another block party at Conseco Fieldhouse, rejecting 13 shots after 19 in Game 2. Jermaine O'Neal was slowed by an injured left knee and scored 11 points.

"Even though we're out there trying to kill each other, I'm concerned about him as a friend," Rasheed Wallace said of his former Portland teammate. "I asked him before the game how he felt. So he must have felt good enough to play."

Austin Croshere, the hero of Game 4, was ineffective, missing all six of his shots. He made two free throws. Indiana shot just 32.9 percent.

Rasheed Wallace made two free throws and a baseline jumper during an 8-0 run with 5:47 left that put the Pistons in control, 72-59.

Chauncey Billups drives on Jamaal Tinsley in Game 5. Injuries to Tinsley and Jermaine O'Neal hurt the Pacers down the stretch.

KIRTHMON F. DOZIER

THE PLAYOFFS

Bring on the Lakers! Ben Wallace slams over Austin Croshere with 11 seconds left to seal the Game 6 victory.

KIRTHMON F. DOZIER

THE THIRD SHIFT 86

69 PISTONS ROUND 3 GAME 6 SERIES 4-2 PACERS 65

Westward 'fro

Gritty Pistons deck Pacers, will play glitzy Lakers for NBA title

By Mitch Albom

AUBURN HILLS *(JUNE 1, 2004)* — All night long they had been trying to snare the only thing that mattered, a lead. At one point, it was as far off as a ship on the horizon. Slowly, they swam in, clipping away, a point here, a basket there, until finally, finally, in the fourth quarter, they reached sea level.

A tie at 54 points. A tie at 57. A tie at 59. A Chauncey Billups three-pointer. A Ben Wallace turnaround. A Tayshaun Prince block. Whatever was in the arsenal, it was coming out now. Richard Hamilton took a forearm to the face, hit the deck, got up and made two free- throws. Rasheed Wallace saw a missed shot, flew in and slammed it down, falling on his butt.

And at last, when the sweetest sound in their world was heard — a winning buzzer — this wrestling match was finally over, and all the misses, clanks and air balls were behind them, and they looked up and saw the blessed digits on the scoreboard. They leapt.

And confetti fell.

It fell on the players, it fell on the fans, it fell on all those familiar old faces — Vinnie Johnson, Joe Dumars, Bill Laimbeer, even Chuck Daly — in the building for just this occasion.

Welcome back, my friends, to the show that never ends — it just takes a hiatus for 14 years.

June basketball — championship basketball — is here again, honking the horn like an old high school buddy in his familiar sports car, top down, music blaring, harkening back to the days when we all had more hair and more energy, and this same blue-collar franchise did battle with the mambo kings of glitz, the L.A. Lakers.

Rev up the engines.

Bad is back.

An off-balance Richard Hamilton goes to the basket against Ron Artest in Game 6 at the Palace. Hamilton scored 21 points to help Detroit clinch the Eastern Conference title.

MANDI WRIGHT

On an ugly night of basketball, when they survived a first half suitable for framing — if your frame is a garbage can — the Pistons finally managed to knock out the No. 1 seed in the East (Indiana), their former coach (Rick Carlisle), an aging superstar (Reggie Miller), a budding superstar (Jermaine O'Neal) and the defensive player of the year (Ron Artest). And when it ended, the Pistons wiped their jaws, then licked their chops.

"This was crazy, man," Hamilton said when this was finally over and he had scored a game-high 21 points and survived a blow to the face from Artest that left him woozy. "This whole series was an all-out war."

Bad is back.

"This game felt like it took forever," guard Lindsey Hunter said. "It was bang, knockdown, ugghh."

Well put. What was that final score? 69-65?

I don't want to say that it was bad, but the rim was often the best player out there.

But the question on nights like these is always readiness. Who is ready to seize the moment and who is ready to go home? For much of Game 6 at the Palace, both teams played like the latter. The Pistons missed 26 of their first 31 shots. They clanked from the inside more times than a piggy bank penny. Jump shots weren't falling. Lay-ups weren't falling. Passes were stolen. All hands were on deck. And all hands were cold.

Had the Pacers been a better team — or even a more experienced one — they would have exploited this and had a 25-point

THE PLAYOFFS

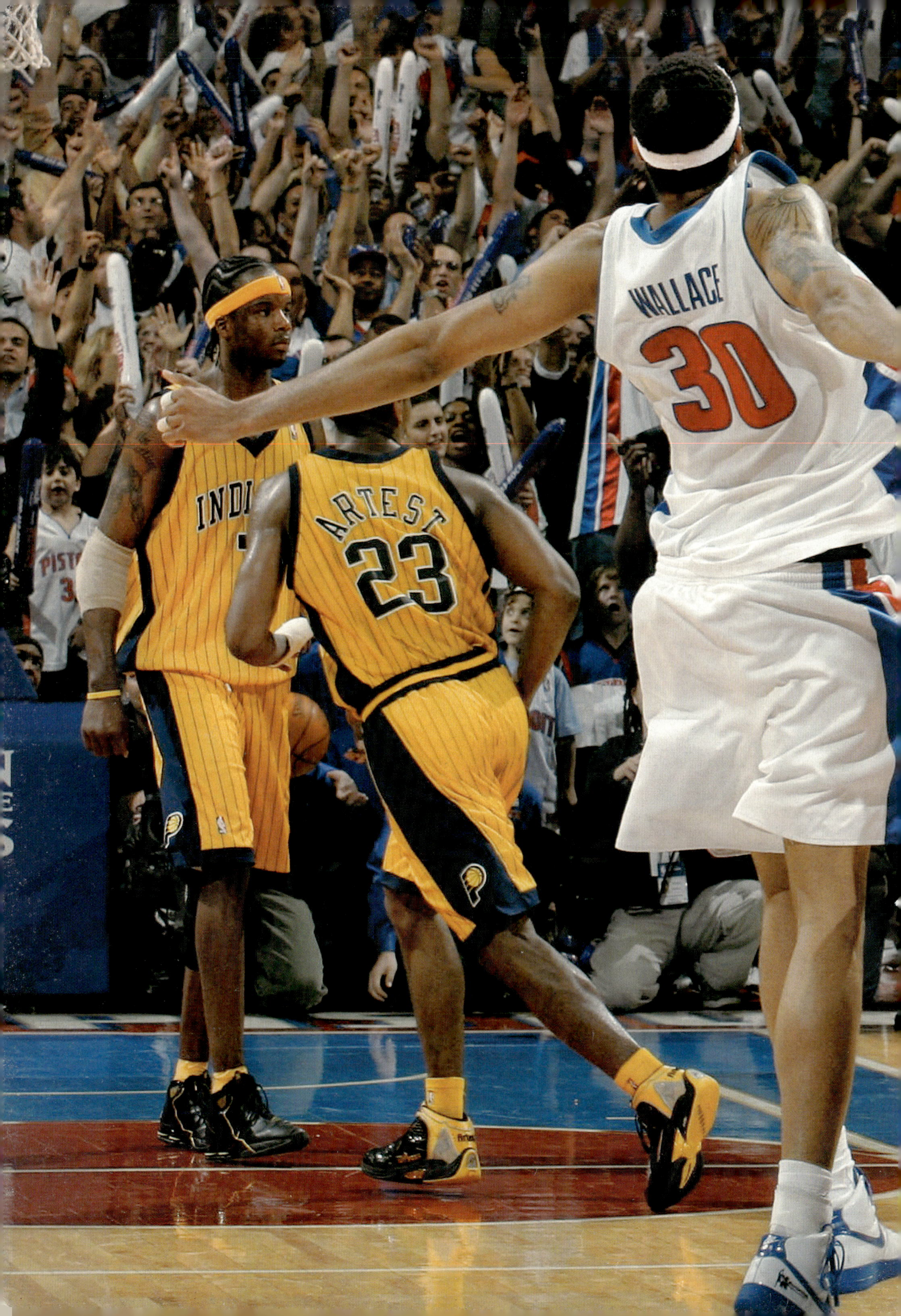
WALLACE
30
ARTEST
23

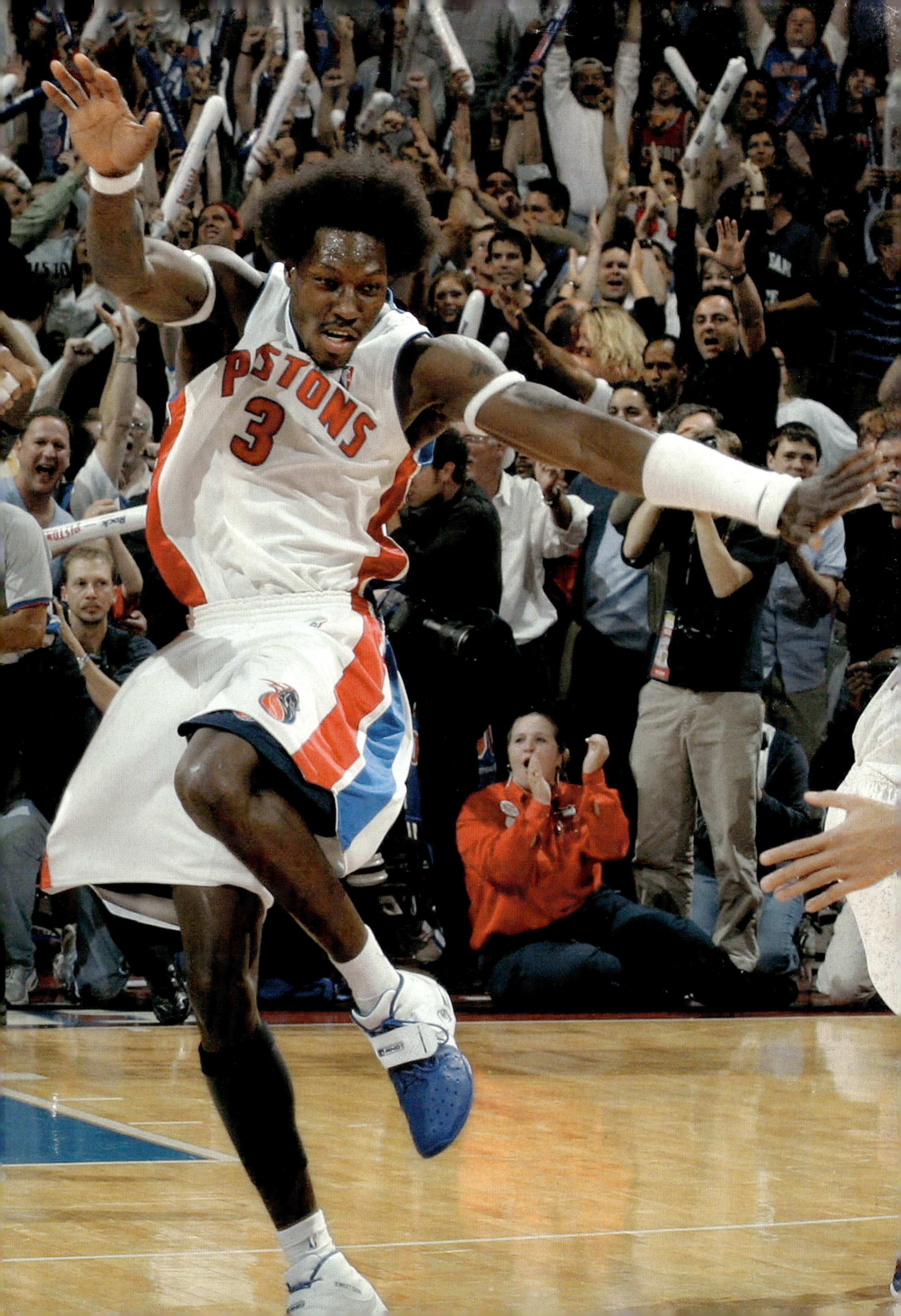
PISTONS
3

Photo on previous pages by JULIAN H. GONZALEZ

Ben Wallace and Rasheed Wallace perform the last on-court dance the Pacers would see. Detroit eliminated former coach Rick Carlisle and the Pacers in six games.

lead by halftime. Instead, Indiana went on long droughts of its own. The Pacers hit just one basket in the first nine minutes of the second quarter. And the distance between the teams for much of that arid section remained nine points, hardly insurmountable.

In the second half, the game tightened. And even though the Pistons didn't reach 50 points until 10 minutes were left, Indiana was within arm's reach the whole time. A Billups three-pointer tied the game at 54, and from that point, it was a drag-down, knock-over, parched-throat crawl to the finish.

OK. So it wasn't art. People said that about Andy Warhol, and he sold a lot of paintings.

Bad is back.

This was a huge moment for Larry Brown, hired one year ago. He did the job — defeating the Nets in the Eastern Conference semifinals and the Pacers in the finals. There will be no ghost of Rick Carlisle.

Bad is back.

How did the Pistons get here? Defense. Rip. Rasheed. More defense. They did it by holding Artest to abysmal shooting all series and by holding O'Neal to mortal status. They did it by adjusting to Carlisle's adjustments (Austin Croshere in the starting lineup, Artest playing tight on Hamilton), they did it by blocking one of every eight Indiana shots.

But mostly they did it with a focus that narrowed when the winning was at hand. They might still make mistakes, these Pistons, but they do learn from them. Having dropped Game 4 in Detroit, they took stock and shook away any cobwebs of complacency. A first half like they had in Game 6 might have sunk another team. Heck, after a first half like that, some teams wouldn't bother coming out for the third quarter. But they hung in, and when Ben Wallace dunked the final two points and the crowd came unglued, it was over. They were there.

Bad is back.

JULIAN H. GONZALEZ

Tayshaun Prince scored just seven points, but made two of the biggest plays of Game 6. He blocked Al Harrington on this late fourth-quarter shot, then made a jumper with 46 seconds left to give the Pistons a 67-61 lead.

4 for the money

A four-point Pistons possession late in the game broke the final tie. What happened:
- Ron Artest was charged with a flagrant foul after striking Richard Hamilton in the face with a forearm with 3:57 left.
- Hamilton made both free throws. Score: 61-59.
- The Pistons retained possession on the flagrant-foul call, and Rasheed Wallace followed a Chauncey Billups miss with a tip dunk. Score: 63-59.

RIP IT UP

Richard Hamilton's shooting statistics in the conference finals:

	FG	3PT	FT	PTS
Game 1	10-20	0-2	3-3	23
Game 2	8-14	0-0	7-8	23
Game 3	7-19	0-2	6-8	20
Game 4	10-24	1-3	1-2	22
Game 5	12-22	1-2	8-8	33
Game 6	7-15	0-0	7-8	21
Totals	54-114	2-9	32-37	142

Photo on following page by KIRTHMON F. DOZIER

Ben Wallace celebrates with the Eastern Conference championship trophy. "It's tough to put this into words," Wallace said of entering the Finals. "It's a great feeling to be able to compete for something you've always dreamed of."

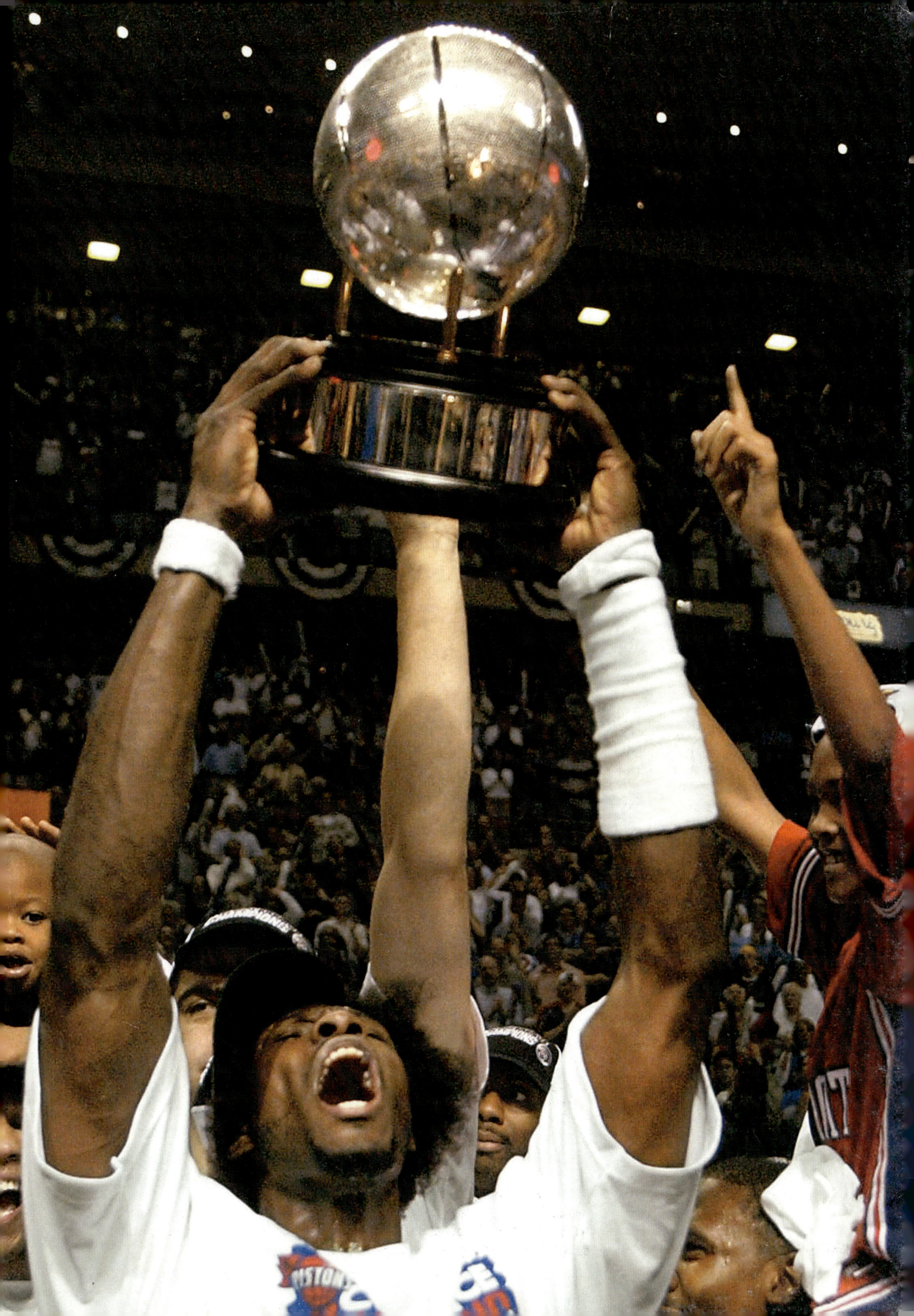

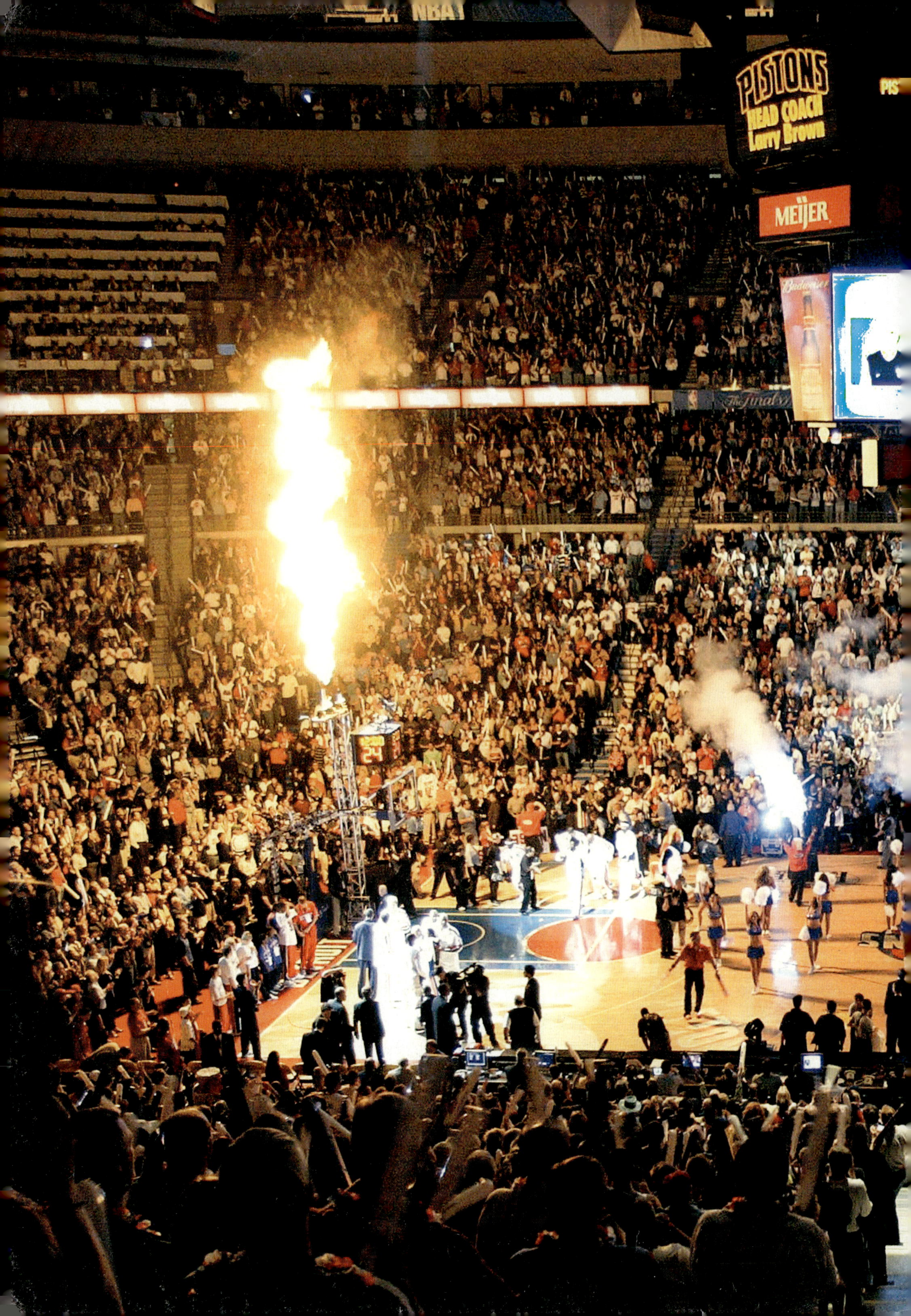
NBA
PISTONS
HEAD COACH
Larry Brown
MEIJER
The Finals

THE FINAL SHIFT

THE FINALS

America's team?

Expectations are so low, the Pistons can't help but exceed them

Palace fans reach to give Ben Wallace five. The Pistons were being picked by numerous national writers to lose in five games to the Lakers.

CHIP SOMODEVILLA

By Jemele Hill

Imagine if that psychotic Green Goblin had beaten the tar out of Spider-Man. Imagine if the princess had told Shrek: "Sorry, I'd rather be with the evil, short guy."

In the movies, good guys almost always win. But that isn't the case in basketball.

If the NBA Finals were determined by the principles of movie justice, the Pistons would be the overwhelming favorite.

The Lakers are the kings of strife; the Pistons are the kings of nice. The Lakers are fat cats; the Pistons are orphans from the wrong side of the tracks.

But here in real life, hardly anyone outside of the Palace thinks the Pistons have a shot at humbling a team whose mystique rivals that of the New York Yankees and Dallas Cowboys.

And that is the Pistons' greatest advantage in this series.

"We love that," Chauncey Billups said.

The Pistons and Lakers split two games in the regular season before the Pistons acquired Rasheed Wallace in a trade.

Like all underdog teams that face dynasties, the Pistons have been crowned the people's champions.

Their blue-collar work ethic, dedication to defense and rebounding, selflessness and lack of superstars have had a charismatic effect on the public.

Lots of fans outside Michigan are rooting for the Pistons to dethrone the team that has won three of the last four NBA titles.

Asked if the Pistons are the people's choice, Shaquille O'Neal said: "Of course they are. Everyone wants to see us falter. I just think that sometimes they think that we're the Yankees of basketball.... We have to do what we're supposed to do. I'm always supposed to win."

But those people don't have to contend with O'Neal, Kobe Bryant, Karl Malone and Gary Payton — four likely Hall of Famers who give the Lakers their undeniable star quality.

The Pistons will be charging up a hill in this series. But they're headed for Hollywood, so it's understandable why they think a surprise ending is within reach.

THE FINAL SHIFT 94

STORYLINES
Hot topics of the Finals

THE COACHES

The Lakers' Phil Jackson and the Pistons' Larry Brown are two of the most successful coaches in NBA history. But that's like saying Wolfgang Puck and Mrs. Fields are two of the nation's most successful chefs. It's technically true, but they don't work with the same material.

Jackson takes over teams on the cusp of a championship, and he helps them build the mental toughness to finish.

Brown takes over teams on the brink of extinction, and he helps them develop the physical skills to stay alive.

Brown convinces the girl she's beautiful. Jackson swoops in and marries her.

Jackson has had at least two Hall of Famers on his roster for 13 of his 14 seasons. And not just any Hall of Famers — Michael Jordan, Shaquille O'Neal and Kobe Bryant are in the Hall of Fame's Hall of Fame.

Until 2003, when the Pistons hired him, Brown had never inherited a winning team. Yet Brown has had a winning record in 28 of 32 seasons.

LAKERS DON'T EXPECT TROUBLE

Defense, defense, defense. It's all the Lakers have heard about Detroit, but the Lakers already beat one very defensive team in the playoffs.

The Lakers dispatched the defending champion San Antonio Spurs in the second round.

The Spurs tied Detroit during the regular season for fewest points allowed by an opponent with 84.3.

"I can't anticipate," Jackson said, "they're going to be any better than San Antonio. It's going to be a good defensive team, but we don't think they have better shot blockers, better rebounders or anything else better than San Antonio had."

KOBE AND THE COURTS

Bryant is 25 and an established superstar.

But he has played the entire season with the possibility that this will be his last. In the summer of 2003 he was accused of rape by a woman at a resort near Vail, Colo., and he was charged with felony sexual assault. Bryant has pleaded not guilty. While admitting he had sex with the woman, Bryant, who is married, said it was consensual.

If convicted, Bryant faces four years to life in prison and a fine of up to $750,000.

The case forced Bryant to travel back and forth to Colorado for court dates. If it ever distracted him on the basketball court, he never let on. Some of his best performances came on days he had flown from the courtroom to a game.

Bryant didn't face more hearings in Colorado until after the Finals.

KOBE AND RIP

Bryant was a superstar player at Lower Merion High in a Philadelphia suburb.

About 40 miles away in less-affluent Coatesville, Pa., Richard Hamilton was becoming a big-time player at Coatesville Area High.

Bryant and Hamilton got to know each other through AAU basketball and by virtue of reputation. They were high school seniors in 1996, when Bryant led Lower Merion to the Class AAAA state title and became the state's all-time scoring leader with 2,883 points.

Both made it to Magic Johnson's Roundball Classic at the Palace that year as high school All-Americas.

Eight years later, they faced each other on the biggest basketball stage in the world.

Bryant told the Orange County Register: "We've played against each other so many times. Very good friends in high school. Still good friends to this day. It's going to be a good challenge."

LONGSHOTS

BetWWTS.com, an offshore gaming company, made the Lakers an overwhelming favorite to win the title. The odds are 1-7 (i.e., win $1 for every $7 bet). The Pistons are listed as 11-2 longshots to win the title.

BAD BOYS VS. SHOWTIME

The first time the Pistons played in the Finals, in 1988, their home was the Silverdome, and they lost the series. The next season, they played at the Palace, and they won.

The opponent both times was the Los Angeles Lakers, the dominant team of the 1980s.

The '88 Finals went seven games, with the Pistons losing the last two at Inglewood, Calif., by a total of four points. In '89, the Pistons swept the Lakers, whose strength was sapped by injuries.

These were the teams of Isiah Thomas, Joe Dumars, Bill Laimbeer and Vinnie Johnson for the Pistons, and Kareem Abdul-Jabbar, Magic Johnson and James Worthy for the Lakers.

US VS. THEM

It's Us vs. Them now, the Pistons vs. the Lakers, Motown vs. Tinseltown. Here's how it stacks up:

Phil Jackson invokes the power of Zen.
The Pistons invoke the power of Ben.

They have the Mailman.
We say, "What can Brown do for you?"

They have the O.C., where wealthy swingers lead the wild life.
You mean that doesn't stand for Oakland County?

They look kind of plastic after all that Hollywood nipping and tucking.
We have Rip Hamilton and his mask.

They have Derek Fisher.
We have Lindsey Hunter.

They have Tobey (Spider-Man) Maguire for a celebrity fan.
We have John (Spider) Salley.

By Free Press sports staff

The Pistons' Rip Hamilton and the Lakers' Kobe Bryant — whose rivalry dates to high school — hug before Game 1 in Los Angeles.

87 PISTONS ROUND 4 GAME 1 SERIES 1-0 LAKERS 75

Take that, L.A.

Pistons' 'D' makes opening statement

By Mitch Albom

HERO OF THE GAME
Chauncey Billups, whose 22 points led four Pistons in double figures.

GOATS OF THE GAME
Lakers starters not named Shaq or Kobe: Karl Malone, Gary Payton and Devean George combined for 12 points.

NUMBERS
20: How many points Shaq had averaged in this playoff year — and how many he scored in the first half of Game 1. He finished with 34, his high for the playoffs.

59: Combined points for Shaq and Kobe (25), or 79 percent of the Lakers' total.

39.7: The Lakers' shooting percentage (29-for-73). And they ripped on the Pacers for hitting less than 40 percent in the previous series.

TALKING
■ Pistons president Joe Dumars: "I think we've gotten their attention now."

TWO CENTS
The first one's nice, but it doesn't mean anything unless you win the last one.

LOS ANGELES *(JUNE 6, 2004)* — They arrived like the plumbers called to fix the movie star's sink. Barely noticed, anonymous but for their uniforms, they knelt, took out their toolbox and went to work. And by the time the game was finished, water was all over the place. And the Pistons sloshed out promising to come back and fix it Tuesday.

Beatable.

When the buzzer sounded, the Pistons had done to the Lakers what many thought they wouldn't do in four. Knocked them down a game, and maybe down a peg.

It was Pistons 87, Shaquille O'Neal 75. On this night, the rest of the Lakers — with the exception of Kobe Bryant, who scored 25 — were as invisible as the key grip and the gaffer.

You can thank the Pistons' defense for that. The Pistons came, they saw — and they didn't break down in terror. Forget the pressure. Forget the reputation of their opponent. Forget the movie stars or the Laker Girls. The Pistons brought their defense with them, as they always do, and they were pleasantly surprised to find some space between them and the men defending them for once.

"Nervous?" Ben Wallace said after the Pistons' first game in the NBA Finals since 1990. "Well, I think my first jump shot was a 15-footer that went 13 feet. But we relaxed faster than they did. And after a while it became a regular game."

A game in which they got points from everyone — including 22 big ones from Chauncey Billups — a game in which they bothered Bryant just enough, shut down Karl Malone, virtually erased Gary Payton and held the Lakers' bench to four points.

"A lot of guys came up B-I-G," Rasheed Wallace said.

He's R-I-G-H-T.

And in the final minutes, it was the Pistons who looked at home. Meanwhile, O'Neal, the one unstoppable force all night, watched with a "What's going on?" look on his face.

Can you blame him? The Lakers had not lost a playoff game at home all season.

Until now.

Highlights? How about Tayshaun Prince, after the Lakers had cut the lead to six points, hitting a huge three-pointer with just more than four minutes left? How about Ben Wallace shaking off his air ball to hit a big jumper to give the Pistons a seven-point lead and a tip-in to make it 10? How about Richard Hamilton, thwarted from his usual offensive night, taking a charge for an offensive foul in the final five minutes?

"If someone had told you that Rip Hamilton would be 5-for-16 tonight, what would you have said?" Billups was asked.

"I would have said we'd be all right," he answered. "We got other guys who can score on this team."

The Lakers? Scoring 75 points? Shooting less than 40 percent? Losing?

"It's a seven-game series," Bryant warned.

"I don't know if we could ever defend better," Pistons coach Larry Brown said.

For this team, that's saying something.

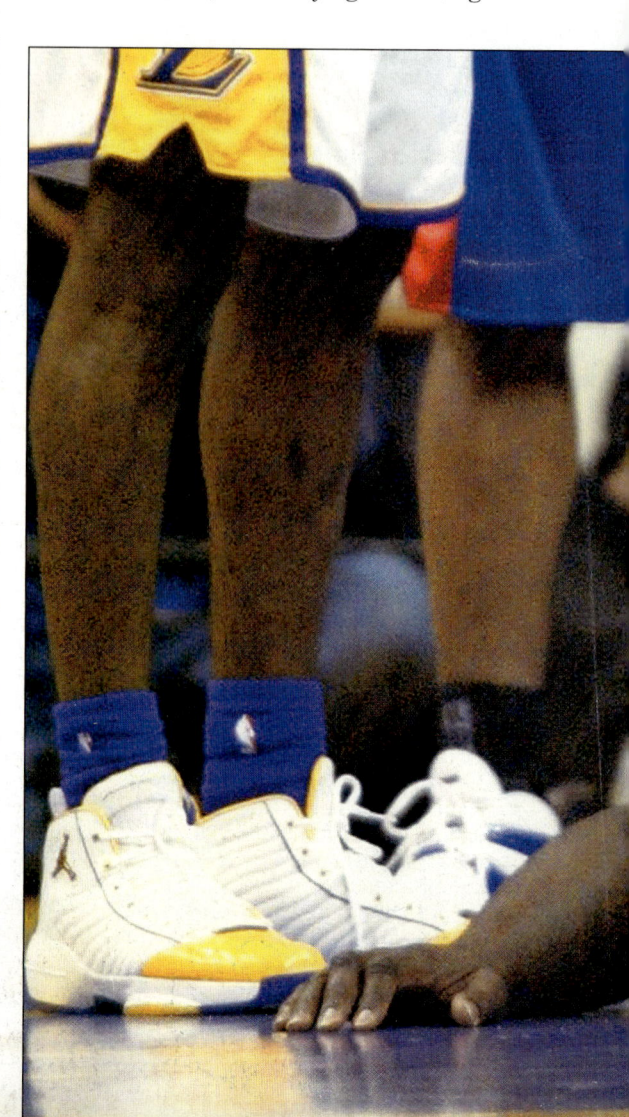

THE FINAL SHIFT 96

Shaquille O'Neal dwarfs Chauncey Billups, who scored 22 points in Game 1 and started his drive to the Finals MVP award.

MANDI WRIGHT

Three-sport standout

In the fog of a playoff victory this season, Rasheed Wallace shouted, "How about them Pistons?!" Well, how about 'em? In the heady world of Bill Davidson's sports empire, they're just another team.

The Shock is the defending WNBA champion.

A day after the Pistons' Game 1, the Tampa Bay Lightning won the Stanley Cup.

The Pistons? Title No. 3.

"I don't know that it gets any better," Palace president Tom Wilson said. "The stars have to align."

In the spring of 2001, the Pistons finished 32-50, the Lightning had the second-fewest points in the NHL and the Shock was on its way to a tie for the worst record in the league.

What were the chances that three teams with such abysmal records would reach the top of their leagues in just three years?

It's quite a coup for Davidson, and we all know how much it warms the heart when a billionaire makes good. For now, Detroit gets to enjoy only part of the dynasty. But Davidson is only 81. Maybe some day he will buy the Lions.

By Michael Rosenberg

Photo below by KIRTHMON F. DOZIER

The Lakers' Shaquille O'Neal was felled to the Staples Center floor by a Detroit foul in Game 1.

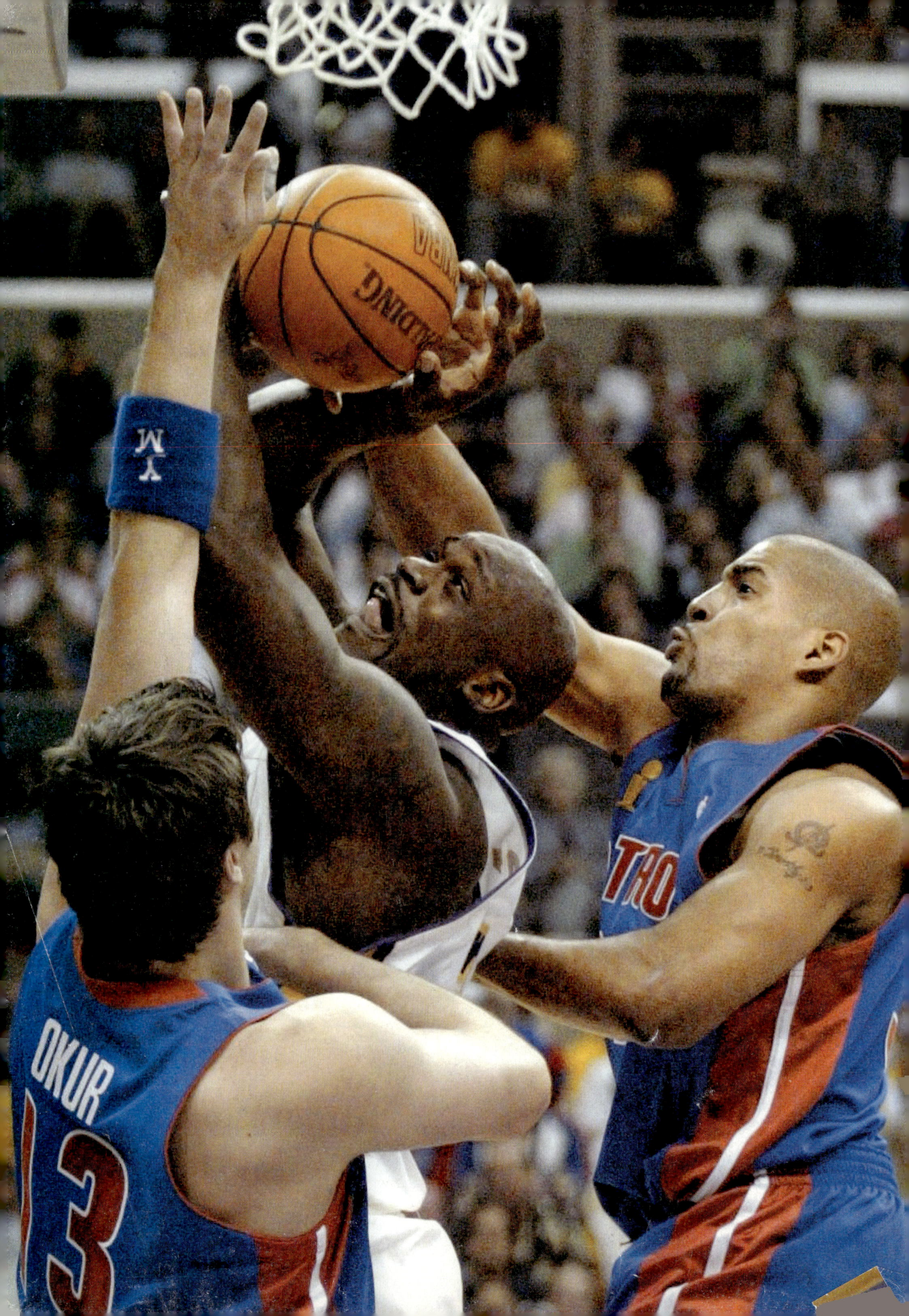
OKUR
13

As good as it gets

At courtside in L.A., the stars are overflowing

Snoop Dogg was loyal to his Lakers, but he watched the Pistons go wild at the Staples Center.

By Michael Rosenberg

LOS ANGELES — Jack was here. But Jack's always here. Denzel was here — we don't like to use last names here in Hollywood — and so were Jackie Chan, Disney chief executive Michael Eisner, Matthew Perry, Star Jones and Jeff Goldblum — and that's just a tiny, partial list.

An NBA Finals game in L.A. has more star power than any other sports event — maybe any other event, period, outside of award shows. At Pistons games, people go nuts over Kid Rock. In L.A., there are a hundred Kid Rocks.

Celebrities are just like the rest of us, except wealthier, occasionally more talented, almost always more self-absorbed. But no matter how jaded you are, there is something surreal about seeing people you know, but have never met, walking in front of you, latte in hand.

The celebrity percentage is simply amazing. And I'm not even talking about sports celebrities like Kareem Abdul-Jabbar and Pete Sampras and Lisa Leslie and Magic Johnson, who were all here.

Leonardo DiCaprio was here. I'm not sure if he's a basketball fan or happens to be dating four Laker Girls. But he was here.

Chris Rock was here. "I don't see the Pistons winning... anything," Rock said. "You never know. Shaq and Kobe could get arrested the same day."

Dustin Hoffman was here. Apparently he's always here, too.

At halftime, the stars all go to the Chairman's Room, a club under the stands. I figured I'd use the rest room outside the Chairman's Room to see if I'd run into a celebrity. First person I saw in there? Sylvester Stallone.

This was like a movie premiere, but with a few differences.

At a Finals game, the stars actually stay for the event. They don't just get photographed, then head out the back door so they don't have to sit through another bland movie.

The biggest difference, though, is this: At a Finals game, the stars mingle among the riffraff. It is why games remain the most accessible big-time event in America; Vin Diesel will be surrounded by people you've never seen before (they couldn't all be his bodyguards).

A word here about Jack Nicholson. His Laker fandom is well-known, and because he remains such an acting icon, it's almost like the teams are playing on his court.

Sorry, Jack.

Jack Nicholson was still smiling early in Game 1, but the worst was yet to come.

Photo on previous page by JULIAN H. GONZALEZ
Corliss Williamson, right, and Mehmet Okur sandwich Shaquille O'Neal in Game 1 of the Finals.

99 LAKERS ROUND 4 GAME 2 SERIES 1-1 OT PISTONS 91

The empire strikes back

Wasted opportunity will haunt Detroit... and why didn't Brown order a foul?

By Mitch Albom

Chauncey Billups bows his head during the Pistons' low point of the series, late in their overtime loss in Game 2.
JULIAN H. GONZALEZ

HERO OF THE GAME
Kobe Bryant, whose only three-pointer forced overtime with 2.1 seconds left. He scored 20 of his team-high 33 points in the second half and OT.

NUMBERS
10-2: The Lakers' advantage in OT.

6: The Pistons' lead with less than 50 seconds remaining in regulation.

61-43: The Pistons' advantage in trips to the free-throw line the first two games. So much for those NBA conspiracy theories.

TWO CENTS
It's going to be a red-eye back to Detroit for the Pistons. But then ... get over it. What happens in L.A. stays in L.A. should be their motto.

LOS ANGELES *(JUNE 8, 2004)* — They were three seconds from the top of the castle. Three seconds from a hammerlock on this series. And then Kobe Bryant lifted as high as a man can go without a trampoline, and Richard Hamilton got a hand up but not enough body, and the ball flew toward the hoop with every ounce of Lakers legend spinning a cloud of pixie dust around it. You knew it was going in. You could have closed your eyes and seen it. And when the net had been swished and the crowd had exploded and the game had been tied, this series that had been to that point — despite what everyone else said — really about the Pistons, suddenly really did become about the Lakers.

Their legacy. Their magic. Their reputation.

Their game.

That close.

You can ask a lot of questions — why didn't the Pistons foul Shaquille O'Neal? Why didn't Rasheed Wallace hang on to the inbounds pass with two seconds left? Why did Ben Wallace foul O'Neal on a lay-up when the lead was six? Why didn't this or that? But the truth is, the Pistons had their chances. They had this game in hand. And when Bryant hit that shot with 2.1 seconds left to force overtime, their hands opened as if pried with a claw. And they gave it back.

"This is what we do for a living," Bryant said after that huge shot, the biggest three of his 33 points. "On that shot, I was just trying to back Richard up and knock it down."

He knocked the Pistons down as well. And from that point on, they were in a daze. They might as well not have been out there. Kobe was the hypnotist, running his hands in front of the Pistons' eyes, dangling a watch, putting them in a spell.

Final score: 99-91 in overtime.

Kobe Bryant averted what probably would have been a Pistons sweep when his three-pointer at the end of Game 2 forced overtime.
MANDI WRIGHT

THE FINAL SHIFT 100

Instead of flying home with a stunning and commanding 2-0 lead in the Finals, they are tied in games.

Their game.

That close.

The shame of this is all the Pistons wasted with a few bad plays. They wasted a wonderful comeback from 11 points down. They weathered one of those one-night, star-is-born performances that can kill you in the playoffs, when rookie Luke Walton provided eight assists and seven points.

They survived all that. But they couldn't survive Kobe, who lives for these moments. Bryant scored 14 points in the fourth quarter and overtime. And then — the big shot.

Fans will ask why the Pistons didn't foul O'Neal, who had the ball before Kobe touched it on the final possession. At worst, he makes both free throws, the Pistons are still up one, and the Lakers have no time-outs. At best, he misses one or two, and the Pistons have the ball and a cushion.

"We don't foul in situations like that," coach Larry Brown said. "We just wanted to switch out and be aggressive, but we kind of backed off on Kobe's shot."

"We were lucky they didn't foul," Jackson admitted, perhaps being more candid.

Are the Pistons tied, one game apiece? Yes. Is that better than being down, 0-2? Sure. If we offered you this result when they came out here, would you be happy? Likely. But things change by the minute during the Finals, and what was once just a joy to be there had turned into an expectation. That fast. That quick.

Their game.

That close.

Not so funny

Late-night talk show host Jimmy Kimmel mocked the City of Detroit during halftime of Game 2. "I'm glad the Lakers are winning, because besides the fact that I'm a Lakers fan, I realize they're going to burn the city of Detroit down if the Pistons win, and it's not worth it."

It was apparently a reference to sporadic violence following the 1984 Tigers' World Series victory.

Kimmel's anti-Detroit wisecracks got his show pulled in southeast Michigan — and then across the entire ABC network for one night.

He tried to make light of the situation in his apology. "Somehow, I've become Osama bin Piston there. They're very upset in Detroit." Then he added: "It was a stupid joke, I apologize for making it."

As luck would have it, his show's next scheduled guest was Chris Webber of Michigan's Fab Five fame. He gave Kimmel an Isiah Thomas jersey and a Tigers cap.

Kimmel put on the jersey and said: "I hope this is humiliation enough for me, but I sincerely doubt it."

Webber replied with a laugh: "Yeah, I doubt it, too."

BRYANT'S SHOT FORCES O.T.

A WITH 10.9 SECONDS LEFT in regulation and the Pistons ahead, 89-86, Lakers forward Karl Malone inbounds to center Shaquille O'Neal. O'Neal, guarded by Ben Wallace, steps out above the three-point line.

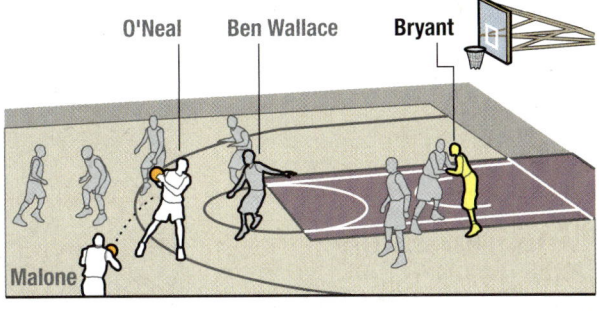

B 10 SECONDS LEFT. O'Neal passes to forward Luke Walton. Walton, guarded by Richard Hamilton, begins to dribble to the right. Lakers guard Kobe Bryant is shadowed by Tayshaun Prince.

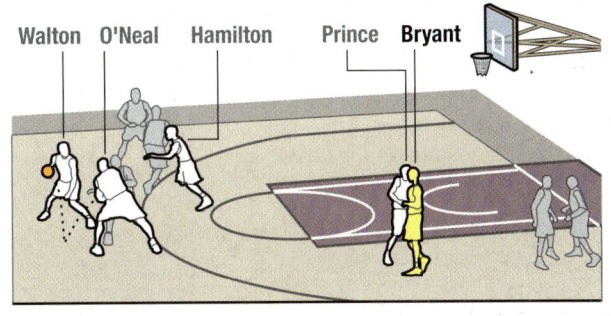

C 7.7 SECONDS LEFT. O'Neal sets a pick on Prince as Bryant cuts to the three-point line. Walton underhands the ball to Bryant. Hamilton switches from Walton to Bryant.

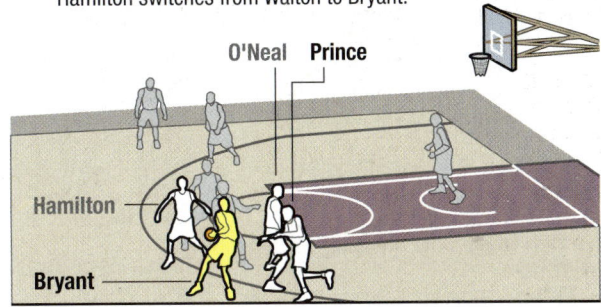

D 3.9 SECONDS LEFT. Bryant dribbles around the arc, closely covered by Hamilton. Ben Wallace elects to stay in the circle instead of doubling Bryant. Bryant rises over Hamilton and scores with 2.1 seconds left.

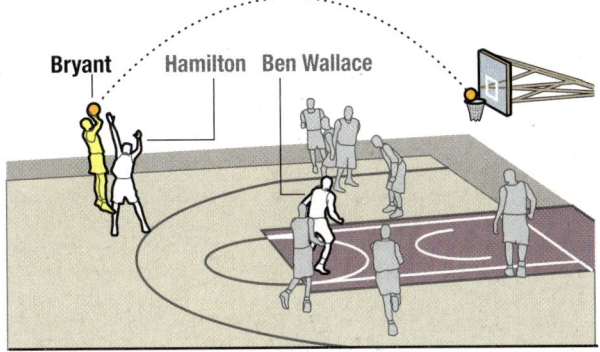

Source: ABC-TV   KOFI MYLER and JOHN W. FLEMING/Detroit Free Press

On the bandwagon

Pistons pride deep throughout metro Detroit

By Free Press staff

Pistons fever is taking hold of metro Detroit. From downtown to Novi and beyond, their pride is showing.

HIGHLAND PARK: SHOP TALK

Carl Pettway walked into Fade Away barbershop the day after Game 3, handslapping everybody in the joint.

"What can you say?" Pettway, 38, asked, as he made his way through the barbershop. "What can you say? . . . It's over. This is it."

Pettway, the owner of Fade Away, was talking about the one thing everybody was talking about — the whipping the Pistons put on the Lakers.

Pettway's barbershop was abuzz with hoops chatter. It was fitting.

The shop has a floor painted like a basketball court. On the wall, Pettway has framed newspapers showing celebrations from the Pistons championship teams in 1989 and 1990. He has a Joe Dumars jersey, Vinnie Johnson socks and John (Spider) Salley high-tops — relics of the players on those squads.

Most of the chatter in the barbershop is pro-Pistons. But as Pettway set up his barber chair, a naysayer emerged.

"He says San Antonio is better than the Pistons," someone shouted, pointing to a customer.

"Don't finish his haircut," Pettway yelled back.

Pettway has no doubts. It's time to add another front-page celebration to his wall.

OAK PARK: DAY CARE DISPLAY

Longtime Pistons fan LaTanya Carter found a way to show support for her home team and give the kids at her in-home day-care center something fun to do.

She and a few of the kids at Tanya's Tots on West 9 Mile near Coolidge created a giant display using Styrofoam cups and blue garland. In bold letters along a long chain-link fence, the cups say, "GO PISTONS 04."

"People honked their horns and shouted hooray" as we worked, said Carter of Oak Park. "This was something a few of them could do with their little hands."

ROSEVILLE: A RUN ON AFROS

Wally Lauer caters to spirited sports fans.

His business, Lauer's Novelty & Costumes in Roseville, sells body paint and colored hair spray, but in the last few months he has sold more than 100 Ben Wallace Afro wigs. He has fewer than 10 left — yours for only $16.95 — and two Super Jump wigs, which are twice as big and sell for $24.95.

Lauer said his wigs are of better quality than most, which means they don't shed. Maintenance also is key, he said. Only use hair spray and a pick to give the wig a fluffy look.

NOVI: SENIOR SPIRIT

Fox Run retirement community in Novi feels partly responsible for the Pistons' Game 3 win. The independent-living center, which has 300 residents, held a pep rally before the game.

They pulled out the ThunderStix and Ben Wallace Afros. They held a free throw and cheering contest. Later, the game was played on the projection television.

Detroit Mayor Kwame Kilpatrick added his stentorian voice to the din backing the Pistons at the Palace.

JULIAN H. GONZALEZ

THE FINAL SHIFT

PISTONS ROUND 4 GAME 3 — SERIES 2-1 — LAKERS — 68 / 68

Kobe who?

Bryant held to 11 points; two more wins for NBA title

HERO OF THE GAME
Rip Hamilton, who scored 31 points, more than any two Lakers combined.

GOAT OF THE GAME
Kobe Bryant, who followed his Game 2 heroics with a one-point first half. He finished with 11, his lowest total of these playoffs.

NUMBERS
14: Shaquille O'Neal's points. He had never scored fewer than 25 in 21 career NBA Finals games.

68: The Lakers' points, their fewest in 561 playoff games during the 50 years of the shot-clock era.

Lakers 88, Pistons 68: The score ABC ran at the end of the game — almost as smart as putting on a "Jimmy Kimmel Live" promo right afterward.

TALKING O'Neal: "If I get my touches, I can still dominate."

TWO CENTS WORTH
Just goes to show you, having the best two players might not be enough when you have the second-best team.

Ben Wallace, left, and Lindsey Hunter battle for a rebound in front of the Lakers' Kobe Bryant during Game 3. The Pistons won, 88-68., and took a 2-1 lead in the best-of-seven series.

By Mitch Albom

AUBURN HILLS *(JUNE 10, 2004)* — Their one guard was supposed to outshine the entire Pistons backcourt. Heck, after Kobe Bryant's miracle shot in Game 2, he threatened to outshine the entire Pistons roster. It was Kobe this and Kobe that. Kobe's destiny. Kobe's greatness. That kind of stuff can give you an upset stomach — especially if you're the other guards. You know, the ones who play against him?

Little wonder then that there were a few extra fist shakes and head nods from Chauncey Billups and Richard Hamilton as they banged down one shot after another. Oh, it might not have been a last-second desperation heave. But you know what? It counts the same. Points are points. Two guards are better than one. And on this night, Billups and Hamilton were twin klieg lights at a shopping mall opening, and Kobe was a 25-watt bulb.

Two get you Two.

The Pistons are halfway to an NBA championship, up two games to one.

"Our guards were phenomenal," Larry Brown said after the 88-68 blowout.

And he was almost understating it.

This was a game in which Bryant, who had THE basket in Game 2, didn't have any baskets the entire first half. None? Meanwhile, Hamilton and Billups were as constant as a jackhammer when you're trying to sleep.

It was rarely close. It was rarely in doubt. Let's see. The Pistons have now handled the Lakers in a Game 1, stared them eye-to-

THE FINALS 103

The Pistons dominated the Lakers because they fought harder for loose balls. Lindsey Hunter beats out Laker Brian Cook for one here.

eye in Game 2 and blown them out in Game 3.

Who was the favorite in this thing again?

"How surprised are you at how much you dominated?" someone asked Brown.

"I'm shocked," he said.

He shouldn't be.

This backcourt performance yielded 31 points from Hamilton, 19 points from Billups, five rebounds and two assists from Lindsey Hunter, and not a single missed free throw from any of them in 14 tries.

"What happened?" someone asked Bryant after he scored 11 points and made only four of 13 shots. "They played excellent defense and we didn't execute," he said. "That's what it boils down to."

Uh, not exactly. You forgot to mention the other guys. Billups? Hamilton? You know? The ones with the 50 points between them?

Two get you Two.

Now. We need to mention the atmosphere on this night.

Well, we might not be home to Jack or Denzel, but we've got our bright lights. Eminem. Barry Sanders. The Yoopers — Izzo and Mariucci. Several of the old Bad Boys — Isiah Thomas, Rick Mahorn, John Salley and Vinnie Johnson — tossed up a ceremonial first tip. Anita Baker sang the national anthem.

And the Pistons picked up the beat from there. They held the Lakers to 37 percent shooting, seven offensive rebounds and four straight quarters of sub-20-point performances.

Here's all you need to know.

Bad delivery

Lakers forward Karl Malone endured a rough time in Game 3, beginning with an incident involving a courtside fan.

The fan heckled Malone during warmups, and ended up being escorted out of the building. The man then filed a report with the Auburn Hills Police Department.

"He looked like he'd had a couple beers," Malone said. "I felt spit hit my face, and I didn't like that too much."

According to witnesses, Malone wagged his fingers and poked the guy in the head. Asked if he touched him, Malone replied, "Maybe I did, but he was on the court, he was in my playing field."

The incident was investigated, but the Oakland County Prosecutor's Office decided the contact Malone made was minor and did not warrant prosecution.

Malone also is severely restricted by a sprained right knee. He was ineffective in the first three games. In Game 3, he scored five points on 2-for-4 shooting.

Darko got in the game, OK? With more than a minute left. And these are the Finals.

My, oh my, things have changed. People are now expecting the Pistons to win, aren't they? In four days, this town went from "thrilled to be here" to "we're gonna be competitive" to "we could push it to six games" to "why shouldn't they beat the Lakers" to "they're gonna beat the Lakers" to . . .

"They better beat the Lakers."

THE FINAL SHIFT 104

Chauncey Billups, though only 6-feet-3, feels like he's nine feet tall as he celebrates a third-quarter basket with Ben Wallace and Tayshaun Prince.

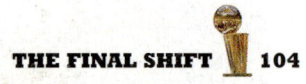

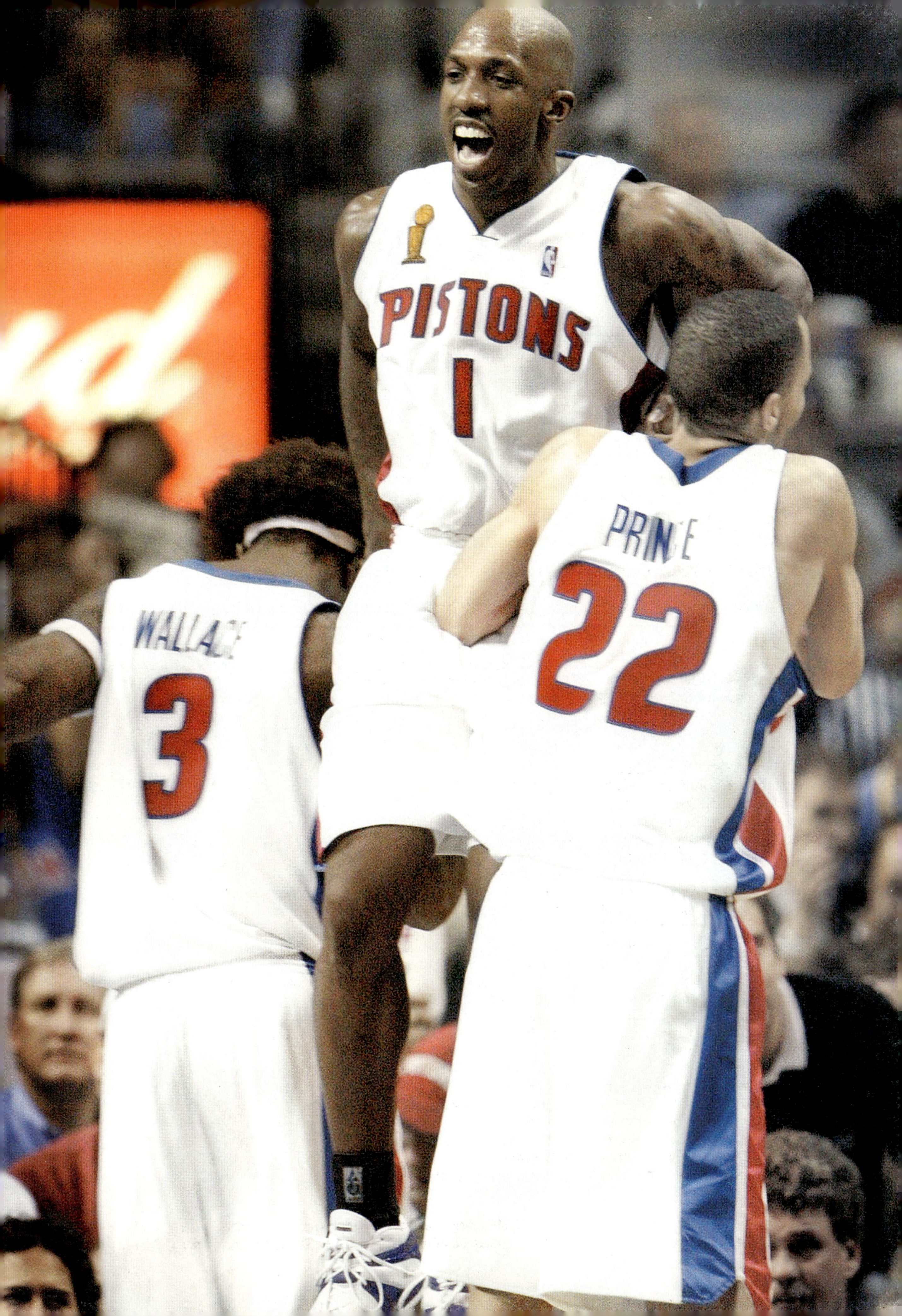
PISTONS
1
WALLACE
3
PRINCE
22

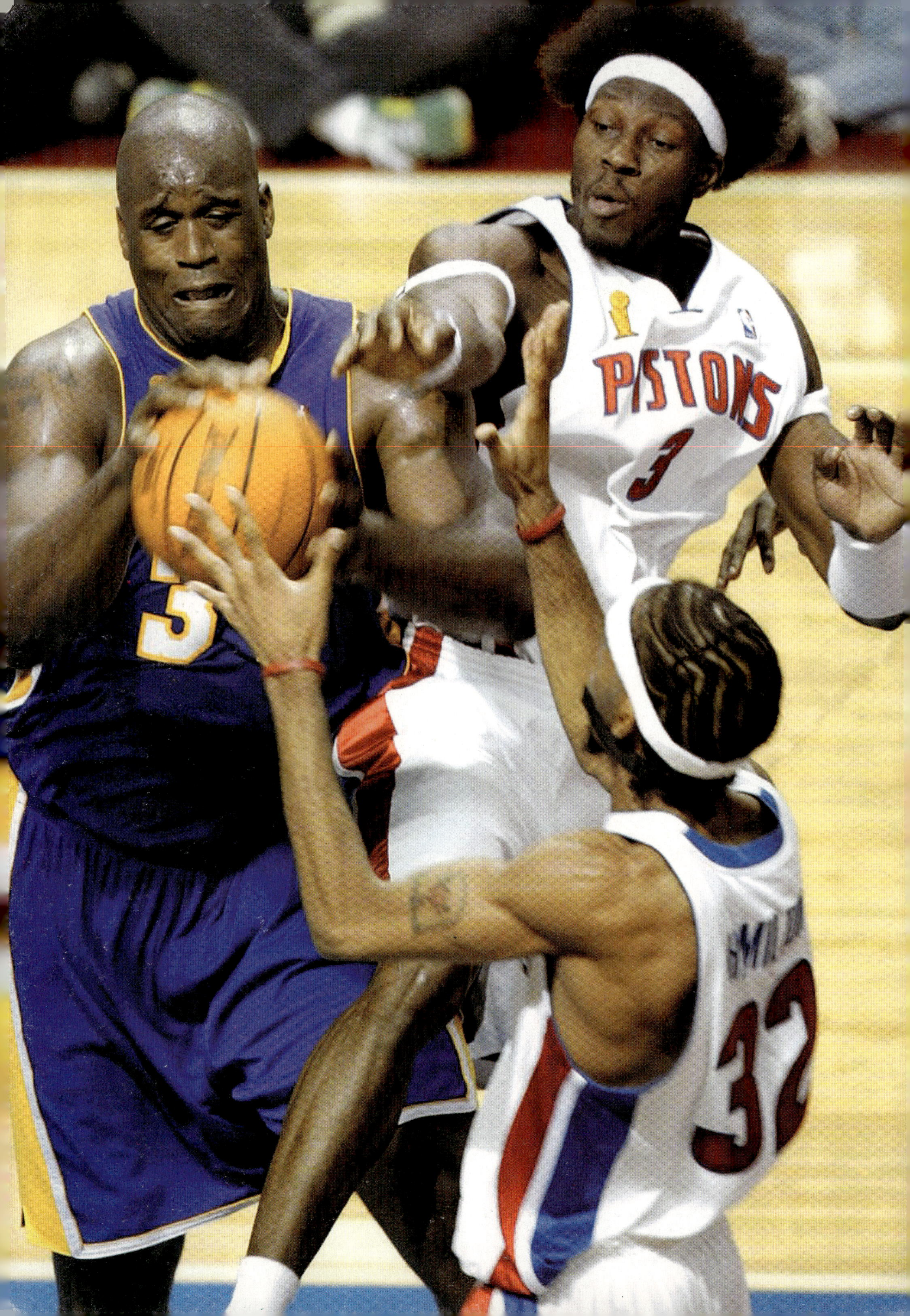
PISTONS
3
32

PISTONS 88 | ROUND 4 GAME 4 | SERIES 3-1 | LAKERS 80

Just one, baby!

Rasheed, Billups put Pistons on doorstep of title

HERO OF THE GAME
Rasheed Wallace scored 26 points.

GOAT OF THE GAME
Kobe Bryant, who got his 20 points but shot 8-for-25 (32 percent).

NUMBERS

0: Teams that have overcome 3-1 deficits in the NBA Finals; the Lakers were the 28th to face it.

2: Lakers who have hit double figures in the series — none besides Shaq and Kobe.

35-20: The Lakers' lead in personal fouls, despite coach Phil Jackson's complaining between games.

TALKING
Bryant: "My shot selection, some of them were good, some of them sucked."

O'Neal: "I know my teammates can play better."

TWO CENTS WORTH
If only the Pistons had drafted Carmelo . . . they might have beaten the Lakers. Hah! Joe Dumars is going to get the last laugh after all.

Richard Hamilton shoots over Kobe Bryant in the first quarter of Game 4. Hamilton scored 17 points. Bryant scored 20 points but shot just 8-for-25 (32 percent). — KIRTHMON F. DOZIER

By Mitch Albom

AUBURN HILLS (JUNE 13, 2004) — The storm arrived, the thunder clapped, and lightning shattered the darkened sky.

And that was inside the building.

Convinced yet? On a night when even the referees' whistles seemed to say, "It's slipping away, Lakers," the Pistons showed their greatest resolve in these NBA Finals, solving the riddle that has befuddled the rest of the league — how do you stop Shaq? — by simply hacking away at his power as if trying to fell one of those beasts in "Lord of the Rings."

He gave everything he had. They took it, then stepped back, exhausted but victorious.

The giant was falling. No team had come back from a 3-1 deficit in the Finals, which is where the Lakers found themselves thanks to the Pistons' stirring 88-80 victory in Game 4 at the Palace.

And while Shaquille O'Neal was simply incredible — 36 points, 20 rebounds — Rasheed Wallace had the game of his Pistons career. He finished with 26 points and 13 rebounds.

Those statistics may not quite match up to Shaq's, but then again, Rasheed has teammates.

"Rasheed was terrific tonight," coach Larry Brown said. "I was so proud of him. We said all along we need him to play minutes and hit his shots. Tonight he showed his value."

Here was Wallace, in this crucial game, doing everything he was brought here to do. Grabbing rebounds. Swiping loose balls. Blocking a Kobe Bryant shot. Spinning on one Lakers defender after another for bank shots, for lay-ups, for fallaway jumpers.

"Just making shots," Wallace

Photo on previous page by MANDI WRIGHT
Ben Wallace and Richard Hamilton try to get the ball away from Shaquille O'Neal during the second quarter of Game 4. O'Neal scored 36 points and had 20 rebounds.

THE FINALS 107

Lakers coach Phil Jackson complained about the referees throughout the Finals. We "want an even shake on the floor and don't want to be playing from an uphill standpoint," Jackson said.

said. "Just making shots."

But it was more than Rasheed. Here was Chauncey Billups, with more crushing three-pointers, and then, on the sweet end of a fast break, rising and spin-slamming for two of his 23 points. Here was Ben Wallace, missing a free throw but getting the rebound and muscling it in for two.

Here was the Pistons' defense, swarming on Gary Payton, Luke Walton, Derek Fisher. And here were those same defenders conceding only one good night, for Shaq, and making pretty much everyone else miserable. Take away Shaq's numbers and the Lakers were just 17-for-57. The pundits call that amazing defense.

Around here we call it Sunday night.

All right. A few words for Shaq. Having tamed the guards and the sentinels, it was time for the

Kobe guarantee?

As the Lakers' Kobe Bryant made his way to the team bus after an 88-80 loss in Game 4, he told an L.A. Times reporter, "I'm telling you right now, we'll win Tuesday."

Tuesday was the day of Game 5.

When asked about the guarantee the next day, Bryant said, "I'll go with that, man. It's fine with me. We don't have a choice."

Pistons to face the L.A. monster head-on.

He began inside, slamming his first basket, rim-rattling his second. He moved slightly outside, hitting an eight-foot jump shot, then a nine-foot hook shot, then back inside for another slam, then a rebound, another rebound, a feed to a teammate for a lay-up and then back inside for another dunk. And that was in the first 12 minutes.

But like a bull in those one-sided bullfights, too many swords eventually lead to wobbly legs. O'Neal could not carry the Lakers all game long, and he tired just enough in the fourth quarter.

For four quarters on the Lakers' most desperate night of the season, the Pistons weathered them, matched them, pulled ahead of them, and, finally, held them off.

"Do you guys feel like it's over?" someone asked Lakers coach Phil Jackson.

"They don't feel it's over," he said. "They just want a fair shake. They want an even break from the refs."

Folks, when they start blaming the referees, it's over.

And Phil Jackson knew it.

100 PISTONS ROUND 4 GAME 5 SERIES 4-1 LAKERS 87

Team works!

Title a perfect fit for lunch-bucket team and city

HERO OF THE GAME
Ben Wallace, who scored 18 and had 22 rebounds.

NUMBERS
1: Uniform number of Pistons guard Chauncey Billups, the NBA Finals MVP. He averaged 21 points, 5.2 assists and just 2.6 turnovers a game.

4: The Pistons' new address, as in 4 Championship Drive.

27: Fouls by each team, so guess the refs were neutral.

1:59: Darko time! At 18, the youngest player ever in the Finals, the rookie was on the court at the end. Now that's a last laugh.

SPEAKING
Joe Dumars: "I felt like we could win this thing even before the season started. I just felt like it was these guys' year to win it."

TWO CENTS
The Pistons — America's Team, the People's Champions — did it the right way. They never stopped working and won it on their home turf. There's only one reason to go back to L.A. now: Disneyland!

DAVID P. GILKEY

The Pistons celebrate their 100-87 victory in Game 5 over the Lakers that ended one of the most surprising NBA Finals in the last half-century. It was a triumph of togetherness over talent, collaboration over celebrity.

By Drew Sharp

AUBURN HILLS *(JUNE 15, 2004)* — They were square pegs squeezed into circular confinements. Their failure to conform was perceived as an inability to succeed.

Chauncey Billups couldn't lead.
Richard Hamilton couldn't learn.
Rasheed Wallace couldn't leave well enough alone.
And Ben Wallace just couldn't . . ..

Each found the right fit in a franchise that eschewed conventionality. And as years of frustration evaporated in a moment of triumph in Game 5 of the NBA Finals, they each assumed a look of stunned amazement.

Billups hugged his coach, Larry Brown, and wouldn't let go..

Rasheed Wallace bounced up and down like an unfettered little kid — this veteran liberated from the weighty burdens of a tumultuous past.

It was time to punch out after an honest season's work.

And despite all the contrary evidence over the previous four games, there remained a sense of disbelief as a year's sweat turned into a moment's tears. Rub your eyes until they're red, it won't change the message that exploded onto the Palace scoreboard: Detroit Pistons — 2004 NBA World Champions.

Raise your lunch pails in salute.

If ever a champion fit the personality of its community, it was these Pistons.

"Against all expectations," said NBA com-

THE FINALS 109

Chauncey Billups, driving around Kobe Bryant, was named Finals MVP. Billups averaged 21 points and 5.2 assists in the series. He also became the first MVP without an All-Star appearance since Joe Dumars, who won in 1989 and then played in his first All-Star Game in 1990.

JULIAN H. GONZALEZ

missioner David Stern during the Larry O'Brien Trophy presentation, "this city believed in this team when nobody else did. ... They proved that fairy tales can sometimes come true."

The bell that tolled for the Lakers was Big Ben. The high-coiffed one flew without the need of wings, snatching destiny from the sky. His fuel was years of blather that there was no place in the NBA for him. But there he was, scoring as well as defending, doing everything prior coaches told him he couldn't do and shouldn't try. He nearly clipped the Palace roof when he soared to slam back an offensive rebound.

"Nobody gave us a chance against these guys, but we knew all along that we belonged," said Ben Wallace, who had 22 rebounds, 18 points and three steals in Game 5. "This is why you play the games. It's a great feeling. There were a bunch of guys on this team who felt they had something to prove. We added a lot of guys over the last couple of years to get to this point. And we took care of business."

The moral of this championship is that you never know what you can do until you try.

History will smile upon this as one of the biggest upsets in NBA Finals lore. And that's not a slight to the Pistons. If anything, it should be proudly displayed as a badge of honor.

It had been 14 years since this franchise scaled to the mountaintop, but it wasn't the passage of time that had made the community's emotions so ripe for ignition. It was the unexpectedness of the triumph.

Customarily, when Detroit teams reached the climactic stage, they were the favorites — the Bad Boys, the Red Wings or the Tigers.

This time, Detroit was a giant slayer. This time, Detroit was the determined underdog.

This time, this quest, was a perfect fit.

Photo on following page by MANDI WRIGHT

It's Wallace X2: Ben and Rasheed put pressure on Shaquille O'Neal in Game 5. Ben Wallace made the Lakers "Fear the 'Fro." He scored 18 points and grabbed 22 rebounds.

THE FINAL SHIFT   110

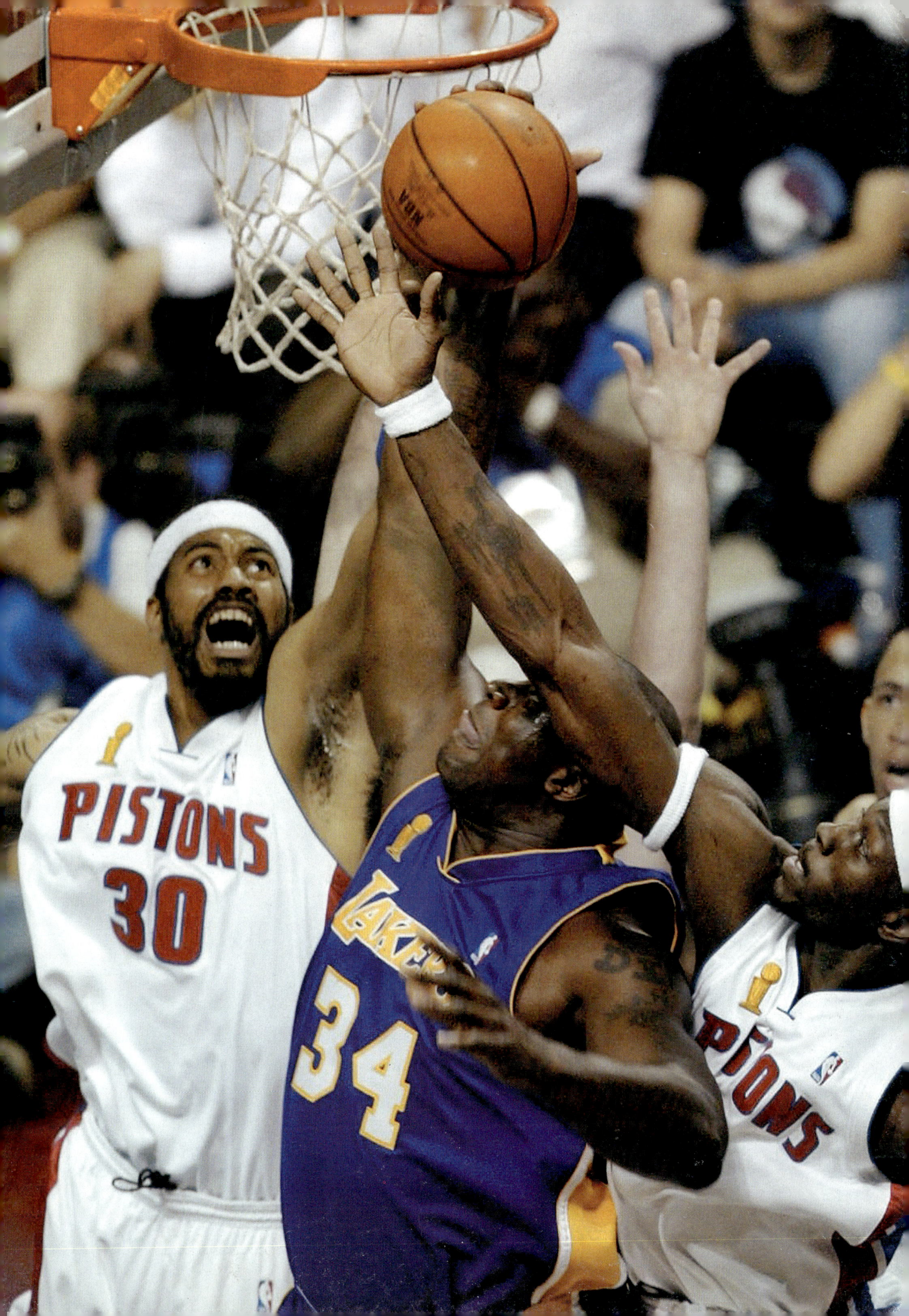
PISTONS
30
34

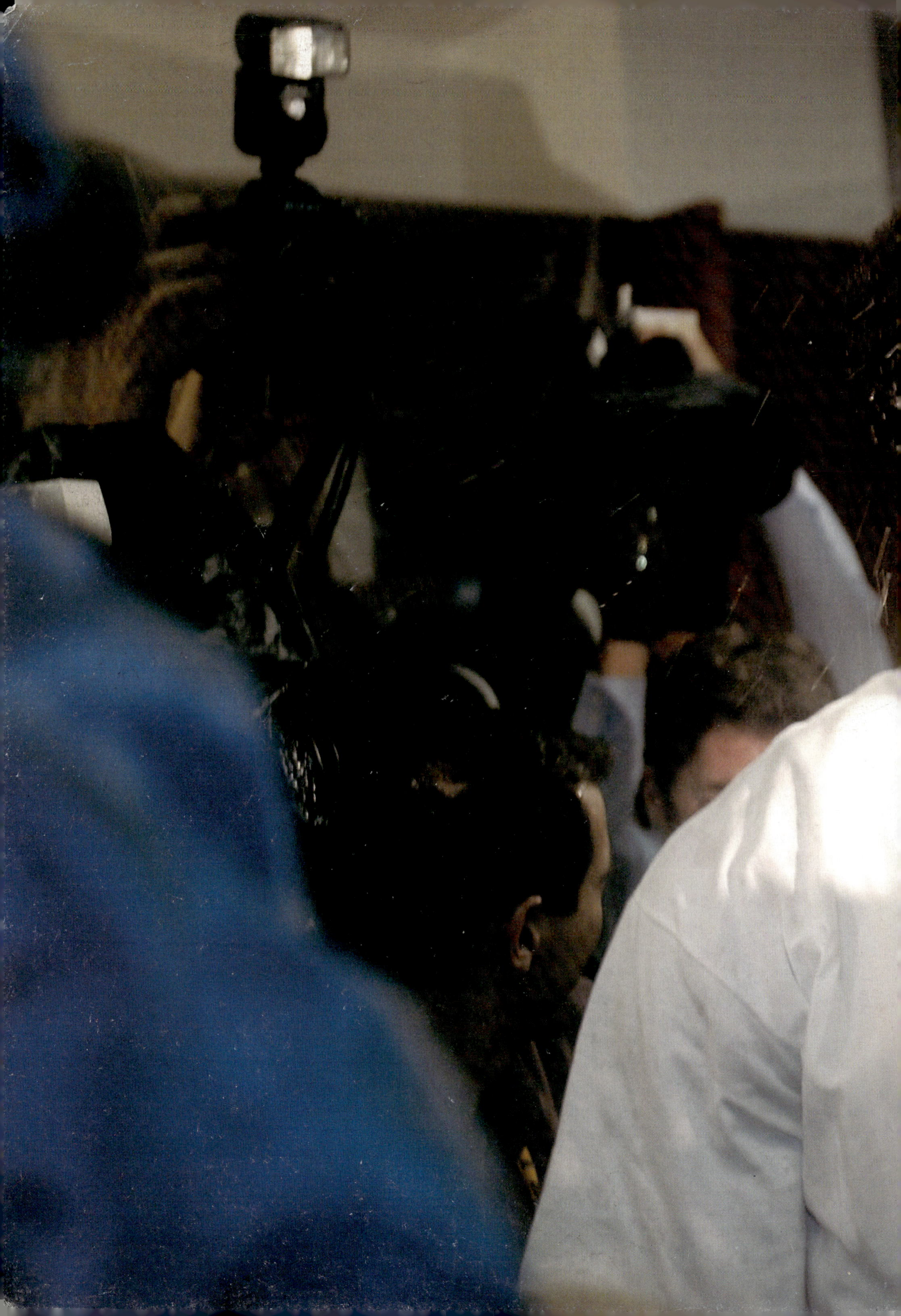

Miracle workers

X marks the spot as Pistons don their crowns

By Michael Rosenberg

AUBURN HILLS (JUNE 15, 2004) — Spare parts and leftovers, unloved and unwanted, the 2004 Detroit Pistons suddenly had nothing but time. As the clock wound down on their improbable championship, Chauncey Billups put his hand over his heart. Ben Wallace danced. Rasheed Wallace shouted. It seemed the world could hear him now.

And then it ended, the fifth and final game of these NBA Finals, and the Pistons rushed the court.

Rip Hamilton hugged Kobe Bryant, his old friend and high school rival, the man he had just beaten on the sport's grandest stage. Kobe congratulated him heartily.

Then came John Salley, straight out of 1990, victory cigar in his mouth. His old teammate Joe Dumars tried to grab the cigar. Salley offered one from his pocket, Dumars took it, and they hugged.

Then Queen's "We Are The Champions" blasted over the loudspeakers, and it seemed like every other championship celebration . . . except here came Ben Wallace, spray paint in hand.

"I've gotta . . . I've gotta," he said.

He ran to courtside, where this team of worker bees had one job left. The NBA had posted 16 numbers at courtside in every playoff arena, signifying the 16 wins needed for a championship.

Every time a team won, it spray-painted an "X" through one of the numbers. The 16th "X" had to be applied.

Ben tried. Almost no paint came out. Nothing came easy to this team, but like a true 2004 Piston, Ben kept at it, painting a circle, and finally a slash, and then an "X," and then, for good measure, he turned it into an asterisk.

Finally, these Pistons had a star. They screamed and danced, all but Larry Brown, who had become the first coach ever to win college and pro titles. Brown held his daughter, Madison.

And then came the trophy. It went to owner Bill Davidson, who now owns the NBA, NHL and WNBA champions.

Then the trophy went to Big Ben, the undrafted superstar, the soul of the team, who held it so tightly, he looked like he would break it in two.

And then they announced the MVP — "No. 1, Chauncey Billups!"

And Hamilton and Tayshaun Prince danced and danced and danced, and Corliss Williamson smiled the world's widest smile, and Lindsey Hunter, back with his original team, never looked happier.

Then Larry Brown hugged his brother Herb, two hoops lifers celebrating their greatest night.

Larry Brown arrived amid controversy a year ago, replacing successful coach Rick Carlisle, demanding that his team "play the right way."

He said it again and again, even as everybody told them they would never win a title together, because none of them were among the league's elite players.

As the confetti fell and the lights flashed, one team was left, the only team with 16 "X's" on the side of their court. They played the right way, Larry. They played the right way.

Rasheed Wallace kisses the Larry O'Brien Trophy. "I don't think we're here without him," Pistons president Joe Dumars said. "No question. I expected him to come in as an All-Star type performer, someone who can impact the game on both ends of the court."

Photo on previous pages by KIRTHMON F. DOZIER

Big Ben Wallace gets a spray of champagne in the locker room. Wallace personified the hardworking mantra of the Pistons. He was usually the last person to leave the court at practice, preferring to spend extra time shooting jumpers.

THE FINAL SHIFT 114

Time capsule

What was going on the year the Pistons won their title:

- Barry Sanders and John Elway went to the head of the Pro Football Hall of Fame's Class of '04.
- "Lord of the Rings" ruled the Oscars.
- "Passion of the Christ" ruled the box office.
- The Red Wings ruled the regular season but flopped in the playoffs, thanks to the Calgary Flames.
- The Lions flopped in '03 but showed off-season signs of improvement, signing Tai Streets and Damien Woody and drafting Roy Williams and Kevin Jones.
- The cicadas came back after 17 years.
- The Tigers showed signs of life for the first time since '87, too, with new star Ivan (Pudge) Rodriguez.
- Janet Jackson showed too much at the Super Bowl. On the field, New England was too much for Carolina.
- Michael Jackson faced molestation charges in California.
- Steroids and college sex scandals gave sports bad headlines.
- The Florida Marlins were the reigning World Series champs, and the Tampa Bay Lightning won the Stanley Cup.
- The Yankees reloaded with A-Rod.
- LSU and Southern Cal shared the NCAA football title.
- UConn didn't share the NCAA basketball titles with anybody.
- Nevada upset Michigan State in the first round of the NCAA, but Michigan won the NIT (and there was plenty of room for the banner).
- TV viewers said good-bye to "Friends" and "Frasier."
- Eaters said good-bye to carbs in an Atkins-friendly world.
- Obstruction of justice is a bad thing, a jury said to Martha Stewart.
- Outkast said "Hey Ya!" to the Grammy for Album of the Year.
- Donald Trump said "You're fired!" to Omarosa & company.
- President George W. Bush and John Kerry were engaged in a long, hot campaign.
- Jennifer Lopez married somebody.
- Britney Spears married some- . . . uh, got an annulment.
- Iraq was a mess.
- Former President Ronald Reagan died.

By Steve Schrader

KIRTHMON F. DOZIER

Rasheed Wallace and Mike James, right, embrace after the Pistons clinched their first title in 14 years. "We are sitting on the top of the world," Wallace said.

Photo on following pages by JULIAN H. GONZALEZ

In the middle of the hubbub at the Palace, Larry Brown celebrates with Madison and L.J., his young daughter and son. Brown became the first coach to win an NCAA title and an NBA title. He won the NCAA one with Kansas in 1988. At right are his bosses, Joe Dumars and Bill Davidson.